Praise for

I Looked Into

"What does it mean to take a life, or to save one? If you've ever done something that shocked or shamed you, something that made you wonder who the hell you are, you will find a kindred soul here. If 'boots on the ground' is on your resume, you'll soon be nodding your head in recognition; however, if military service sounds anathema to you, it's even more important that you get to know Rick Hoppe. The stories he recounts shine a light on some lesser-known aspects of American history, international affairs, and human nature. Hoppe's clean, precise prose is combined with introspection and humility that is rare. He's a noncom Marcus Aurelius—the philosopher who goes to war. A warrior who struggles toward understanding."

—HOLLY PETTIT
Author of *To One Who Lives on the Mainland*; veteran, US Army, 1983–1987

I Looked Into My Soul

by Rick Hoppe

ISBN 978-1-64663-736-2

Published by

 köehlerbooks™

3705 Shore Drive
Virginia Beach, VA 23455
800-435-4811
www.koehlerbooks.com

I
LOOKED
INTO
MY
SOUL

RICK HOPPE

VIRGINIA BEACH
CAPE CHARLES

To Park. Brother, I had to change your name in this book because I couldn't bear the thought of your family experiencing one more second of pain because of me. I'm sorry it took me 33 years to get the courage to visit your grave. I loved you and I know you've forgiven me. Maybe one day, I will forgive me, too

PREFACE

I was in high school during the waning years of the Vietnam War and came to adulthood during the Cold War. I remember the night the Berlin Wall fell, and when the Soviet Union just kind of dissolved. I remember Desert Shield and Desert Storm, when suddenly the American public discovered that there were soldiers and veterans among them and that we weren't demons in human form. I knew as I watched the World Trade Center buildings fall that we would exact revenge, and cynically knew that politicians, in uniform and out, would tack their favorite projects and pet peeves onto the effort. I watched my daughter march off to war, and soon followed her on to my own service in Iraq and Afghanistan. I watched as the politicians refused to heed advice of military professionals and thus threw away all the effort, wasting the money, equipment, and lives that those efforts cost. I watched as we ignominiously pulled out of Iraq and then abandoned Afghanistan and thousands of people who trusted us to keep our word. About 6 percent of the US population are veterans or are actively serving. Almost 8,000 each year surrender to the darkness and take their own lives. Over 15 percent of all suicides in the US are veterans. Every year, hundreds

1

of veterans die waiting for the chronically broken and underfunded Veterans Administration to address their health concerns, and about 20 percent of all veterans suffer from post-traumatic stress disorder. The average American can name all members of the Kardashian family, or the number of songs that Taylor Swift wrote complaining about her love life but has no idea that those who swore to protect them are suffering and dying, alone and instantly forgotten.

I don't know if this book will help anyone understand who we are. All I can do is try.

Throughout this story, names and locations have been changed to protect the innocent, avoid discussing still-sensitive operations, and give respect to both the dead and those who loved them.

INTRODUCTION

*"When you cross the river, you can look back and
see yourself waiting on the other side."*

—Rick's Rules for Life, #17

I 'm sometimes amazed that all this stuff, these stories, really
happened. Well, that and the fact that I'm still alive and managed
to live the life I have. I lived it all, so it's not shocking or amazing
that this was my life and that these were my experiences. Most of
the names and a lot of locations have been changed. Much of this
narrative is still classified or otherwise protected information, but
I also wanted to protect the innocent, give cover to the guilty, and
preserve and honor the dead.

It's only when I try to see my life from the viewpoint of others that
I realize what an extraordinary life I've lived. I've had plenty of time
to sit and think and to wonder how I got here. It's part of the life of a
warrior, all that *hurry up and wait*, which means you aren't supposed
to do anything other than be prepared to do . . . something. That leaves
ample time to reflect on the past and present, and to ponder the future.
Sometimes, when it's just me and the darkness, I wonder.

What series of events had to happen in exactly the right order, at exactly the right time, to result in *this*, whatever *this* is? One wrong word and I would never have married. One wrong move and I might be a quadriplegic in a facility somewhere. One missed bit of timing and I could be in a grave. I'm not second-guessing myself so much as I'm wondering about specific, almost random, threads of life experiences that culminated in the *me* that I see in the mirror. I think about the events, and all I see are snapshots, like a slideshow of my life. Well, for most of it. The cool parts and the funny parts are like watching a series of theatrical trailers, with only the best or most memorable clips shown to the hopefully adoring audience. The really horrifying parts are in full living and dying color, snapping from event to event with no fade in and no transition.

So, what's this about? We've all read autobiographies or memoirs of famous figures, prominent politicians, and well-known military officers. I'm none of these. I'm just a guy who found, through fate or just plain, dumb luck, the place he was supposed to be, doing what he was supposed to do, and perhaps leave the world just a bit better than when I arrived. That's about all we can hope for, in the end.

I'm not rich. You won't recognize my name unless we served together. You probably won't know about the places I've been and won't understand how things could have gone so wrong, and in the end, so right. I'm just like millions of others out there. People who, without plan or calculation, find themselves in a life of service, and I indulge myself in thinking I'm a warrior. It's a neat bit of fiction, maybe a way to rationalize the things that I'm not so proud of. Some title, loaded with noble meaning, to explain to myself who and what I am. What we are—*we*, veterans. We call each other Brother and Sister, and I'm so much closer to some veterans than I will ever be to any member of my family. Because we live out here where reality is, where the latest fashion has an acronym, a stock number, and only comes in shades of green or tan. Where danger is a relative thing and death is just another possibility. Out here, it's just us.

Veterans. We wear the shirts and the hats, and drink in VFWs and Legion Halls, and tell stories that maybe didn't happen to us, but happened to someone and so are true—*ish*. But when we sit around the firepit and all the civilians are gone, and it's just us, the stories take a darker turn. Some stories we only tell each other. Others, well, we don't tell anyone, and one day we hope to forget they ever happened. We speak the names of our dead, and we define ourselves differently, maybe even reluctantly.

Guardians? Warriors? Those sound so damned pretentious. Maybe. For each of us, it's different. Some of us are just *doing a job*. Some of us are trying to *serve our country*. Some of us are just in the military because we *want the benefits*. And, for some of us, all those different things may be true. But, for many of us, there is a need to protect, to draw the line between horror and home. Something maybe a little noble and self-sacrificing. When we talk around that campfire, we don't usually talk about the time before we enlisted. On those incredibly rare occasions when we do, some see a past of no consequence. Some see a life that meant little, a life among people who all dressed the same and played with loud things. I just see my life. Unremarkable, until I compare it to the lives of others. What I do see is a life that is the sum of all my decisions, and the price that is paid for those decisions. No matter how we see our life while we are living it, we all spend the rest of our days paying the price. There is always a price to be paid. Sometimes, that price is barely noticeable. Sometimes, all it costs are small pieces of your soul.

These questions are out there, should you think to ask them. Why do they do what they do? Well, *you* should ask. I already know the answer. I mean, you don't know, and you won't ask. You can't understand. It's not that you are deficient in any way. The raw truth is that you don't have a frame of reference to understand us, understand me. That's fine. I don't understand you, either. Actually, I don't think I want to.

Is a warrior born to the role? Do they grow into it? Are they made? Is it just an accident of timing? I don't know. There are a lot of things that I don't know. Mostly, I don't know the *why* of it all.

Any one occurrence in my life could have moved me onto another path, left me with a little, meaningless existence, a retiree sitting in my garage, building birdhouses and knickknacks for family and friends, and thinking on what could have been. In the end, I'm glad that fate—or Fate, or a deterministic God, or the Great Spaghetti Monster—chose this life for me. For every horror and tear, there were plenty of joys and laughter. I choose to laugh, most of the time. It's only in my dreams that I unwillingly embrace the nightmares.

1

I heard a quote once that always stuck with me. Nietzsche said, ". . . if thou gaze long into an abyss, the abyss will also gaze into thee." I've always liked that quote. Even now, when I know what it means, I like it. The danger is that, well, to be successful, which means to survive, we have to know the monster, that Beast, that lives inside of us. We let it out when we need it and shove it back into the darkness when we don't. The danger is not that we may become the monster, because it's already part of us. The danger is that we may fail to return the monster to his hole, fail to turn our back on it, and even fail to welcome it. So many times, I wonder, am I still human, or have I been consumed by the Beast?

I've seen a lot of things in my life. Terrible, bloody, dark, and evil things. Glorious, soaring, jubilant things. I've seen death and hunger and hate and love and fear and sorrow and joy and blood and birth. I've never, ever turned away from them. They are all threads in the tapestry that makes up my life. I'll tell anyone that there's nothing in this life that I fear. But it's a lie. There's one thing that I've turned away from, that I fear. One thing. One incredibly, scary thing.

Me.

For good or ill, I own this thing that I am. This paunchy and balding guy, with the bad knees and back and high-frequency hearing loss. The guy you don't understand, or the guy you don't want to understand. What you see is whatever you've allowed yourself to be programmed to see. I see a guy who is still ready to run to the sound of guns, and who thinks that dying to protect an innocent is a pretty cool way to go. Deal with it. I'm trying to.

It turns out I've worked really hard to avoid looking at myself. On those rare occasions when I have opened the door and looked inside, it was just a peek. Just a glimpse. I've reached a kind of accommodation with that Beast, where he lives in his world and I live in mine, and he only gets to come out when I need him. When shit goes off the wire and the world starts to come apart, the Beast comforts me, and can save lives just as quickly as he can take them. I try to deny that the Beast is part of me. I can't deny that it's somehow cruelly comforting to know that he's there, and when he's needed, he relishes his time out of the cage I've built. I don't know why I'm afraid of him. After all, the Beast is just one aspect of me. He still scares me. Society has taught me to fear him. I'm so scared that he will come out and I won't be able to put him away again.

In the past, I took that fear to mean that the real me should be feared. Inside, deep inside, the Beast is ugly, and twisted and hateful, so it must be true that the real me was a mirror of my Beast. But I was wrong. That Beast and me, we're just two points of view overlooking the same landscape. You don't know how terrifying it is to acknowledge that.

My life has led me to the brink many times. Times when I didn't know that I could go on. Times when I was certain that I would die, or that I should die. Times when I felt like my mind was tearing itself apart, ripping at the seams like rotten canvas. Times when surrendering to the blank madness would be a blessing. Times when I even wanted to die. Because of the hateful thing that lurked under that friendly exterior. Because of my soul. Because it was dark and light and evil and divine and uncaring and tender and human.

2

I was born without a home. I don't mean to say that I was homeless, or that I didn't have a family. I was born into a family that didn't quite feel like mine, and in a place and time that never quite let me in.

My earliest memory is sitting on a floor in a living room, looking out through a picture window. There were trees and what I now recognize as a road, and a bedraggled lawn. My mother swears that I couldn't possibly recognize it because I was only about one year old when we lived in that particular house, but I recall it distinctly. Even though I don't recall ever having been told what house it was, I can point it out to this day. It's part of the problem, really. Many people get to a point in their lives when they have trouble remembering things. I know I forget things more now than I used to. Little things, though. Where are my car keys? Where did I put my wallet? Why is my phone in the freezer? Those things, things of little consequence. There are things, however, that I would give anything to forget. I tried. I just can't.

My father wasn't around. He was there, but I don't remember much about him being a factor in my life until I was in my teens. And, although I wouldn't want my mother to know this, I don't recall much about her being around either. Don't get me wrong, they were fine people. My mother spent over thirty years as a nurse with a sterling reputation and a deeply ingrained desire to help others. My father, a Korean War veteran, worked for McDonnell Douglas corporation in St. Louis, working on the F-4 and F-15 aircraft projects and on the Gemini and Apollo programs for NASA.

They led our family through a kind of silent example. There were no discussions about principles or morals or ethics, but my parents just lived their lives the way they wanted us to live ours. The result, though probably since my earliest days —of raising a kid by some kind of moral osmosis—was that I lived in a world of my own making. The geeky little kid with the unruly hair and the prominent teeth who thought things that made others wonder about him.

I was born in a rural part of Eastern Missouri. It wasn't exactly the boondocks, but I think the boondocks were just down the road. Grade school came and went. I was neither adored nor despised. I just was. I played and didn't really know what the game was. I laughed and never quite got the joke. Come the summer, my cousins and I got rid of our jeans and shoes and shirts as quickly as we could and spent our days in shorts, running barefoot through probably a thousand acres of farms and ranches and woods.

Suddenly, just before I started school, I came into a kind of awareness of things around me, mostly because of my father. We had to move to Pennsylvania when Dad got transferred, and things changed. The world, that was previously consumed with things and activities to be expected of a rural lifestyle, now had us living in the middle of Wilkes-Barre, Pennsylvania. Gone was the tractor and land clearing and thousands of acres of other peoples' land to run on. Suddenly, I was surrounded by new and different experiences.

All my friends had names that ended in "ski." Everyone's father (except mine) worked in the coal mines. There were often comments about that. My dad coming home at night clean, wearing the standard engineer's clothes of the day, a white, short-sleeved shirt and dark tie. Their fathers coming home in blackened overalls, their arms and hands and faces grimed with coal dust. I didn't understand it but didn't let it register much.

Most of the other kids in the neighborhood decided that, because I was from Missouri, I was a rebel. That worked for me. I tried to live up to that.

It was easy. It's easy to rebel when you don't fit in.

One of the things I remember most is my dad buying me a membership into a kind of book club. Every month or so, I'd get these small books about the space program and stickers that I pasted onto a poster. It got me the reputation of being a bit of a space cadet because that sticker poster and a model of a Saturn V rocket were my proudest possessions. I'd show it around to people, and I was mystified when they didn't see the magic in it. I don't remember what the poster was. Just that it was magic. I learned that the future was a place of endless possibility and hope for humanity. Yet another mistaken impression that I blame on my childhood enthusiasm.

My dad was also a charter member of the Science Fiction Book Club. You know what I'm talking about. The one that says, "Take these seven books for free and we will send you a special book selection each month!" Names that started showing up in the bookshelf were suddenly important to me—Laumer, Norton, Clarke, Heinlein. I remember my mind exploding about possibilities that lay before me. I felt like I had a special window into the future, and it always called to me. It was just like *Star Trek*; that 1960s science fiction series told us that the future, again, was a place of hope and that so many of society's ills would be conquered. I could see myself in that future. And I found out that the rest of the world couldn't, not at the cost of losing their own perceived place on the societal ladder. After all, you measure success by the number of people who are below you.

3

I started school down the street from my house. Actually, it was a couple blocks down the street, then left onto another street. Kindergarten wasn't the trauma, I guess, that it was for some kids. My mother, years later, told me how she was somehow, strangely hurt when she dropped me off at school the first day and I calmly took my book bag, turned, and went into the classroom. It hurt her feelings a little bit because all the other kids were crying because their moms were leaving, but I just walked away without a look back.

I didn't mean to hurt her feelings, but it was kind of a foreshadowing of my life.

Everybody has "friends" in school. They played together at recess, passed notes to each other when they thought the teacher wasn't looking, and hung out after school and on weekends. Everybody but me. The strangeness of that, from all my years of school, was that the isolation or distance was normal. For me. I had kids that I was friendly with. I had kids that I played with. I didn't have friends. I recall being told that I was different. I don't remember who said it, but that person was so very right. I lived in that difference, that undefined "thing" about me that was in the world, just not quite connected to it.

Sometime during my first year of school, some people showed up and put my entire kindergarten class through a variety of tests—weird stuff and normal stuff, multiple-choice tests, and tests that were nothing but horribly boring interviews. Then a couple of weeks or a month after that, there was a meeting at the school for some of the parents. Among those parents were mine and those of my best friend, Joseph Kowalski. We all knew that kids whose parents had to show up at the school were in trouble, and Joseph and I didn't know what we'd done for our moms and dads to have to come to the school. While the parents met with the teacher, the kids played in the kindergarten classroom.

I remember after that meeting, my mom and dad and I walked home together. We got to the house, and I don't remember where my dad went, but my mom sat down at the table in the kitchen and called me over to her. It was a little scary. She took my face in her hands and stared into my eyes. I remember it like it was yesterday. Years later, she told me that she didn't remember that evening in our kitchen. I knew, even then, that something had changed, something important.

The next year, all the kids in the neighborhood either went to that same school or to St. Boniface, the Catholic school. Except for me and Joseph. That first day, we thought that we would just walk to school, but our mothers took us to a corner and a bus came and picked us up.

Joseph and I attended Dodson Elementary School, but we weren't mixed in with other classes. We heard the words "accelerated class" a lot, and we caught hell for it on the playground.

By Christmas, we were writing cursive. By the end of the first year, we were doing all the basic math. The second year, we started learning French and algebra, and they taught us to speed read. We went through drill after drill after drill, forcing us to read faster and faster and testing and testing our comprehension. We competed in French language contests, and after school, I tried to fit back in with the other kids. That worked out fairly well, because at that age, the neighborhood kids didn't care much about what you did at school.

I just felt normal. I wonder what my life would have been like had I stayed in Pennsylvania, but the world wasn't done convincing me I was different.

When I was in third grade, halfway through the school year, my father was transferred back to Missouri, back to the same rural town where I was born. There, I found myself in a regular classroom, and on the first day, I was being chewed out. We had to write our names and the date on a piece of paper and some spelling words. I wrote in cursive. The other kids hadn't learned cursive yet, so evidently, I was wrong, and I was being a *big city show off.* Apparently, it was more important than anything else that I conform, even though it was a huge step back. Even though I was capable of much more. And, because I was capable of much more, I was wrong. I never quite understood it.

Society kept trying to beat that concept into my head. I understood the lessons, but they didn't realize that I was different— that I could never just go along with the crowd solely because they demanded I do so.

4

My family was pretty normal, in their own way. I guess, normal for families of that time and that place. My parents were there, and they loved us. I could tell, but I don't remember ever hearing it at home. They never beat us, never brutalized or belittled us. I was the only boy, with three sisters. One sister was older than me, the other two were younger, and of course, being the only boy, I was different. Again.

And still, I just didn't fit. Oh, I had friends. I played, like all the kids. I ran, like all the kids. I got into trouble, like all the kids. But I was never, really, like all the kids. There seemed to be this bubble, and I was in the world, but never really part of it. As a matter of fact, using the word "part" just made me realize something.

It seemed like I was playing a part. And I always let other people write the script. Because, in those days, in that place, at that time, different just wasn't done. So, I was the same as the others, but I wasn't. I was an observer of life.

I remember so many times, looking at the horizon. I wish I could say that it was symbolic, and that I understood the significance of it. It would sound awfully noble, like "I looked out at the far horizons . . ." No, I just remember looking. I don't remember what I was looking for. Heck, I don't think I even knew what I was looking for. I would sit there with my dog, Buddy, and look out over the valley and fields on the south side of the house. I could hear the whining of the big rigs out on the interstate, a couple of miles away, and I would try to guess what wonders they would see, and the places they would go.

The one time I remember anyone from my family being visible in my memories was around the Fourth of July. My dad would get a catalog from a fireworks company in South Dakota, and we would order thousands of bottle rockets and thousands and thousands of firecrackers. I remember that it was a dollar-fifty for 144 bottle rockets, and we would save up through the year to buy as many as we could. When they came in, we had to go to the train station down by the Missouri River to pick them up. It was a high time.

We had that total carelessness about us that all kids have. We'd have hundreds and hundreds of bottle rockets. Not the wimpy ones that they sell now. The ones that exploded at the end of their flight. We took four-foot-long pieces of copper pipe and made bazookas out of them and had bottle rocket fights. We'd stand twenty yards apart or so and fire these things back and forth. I won often enough, for certain definitions of *won*. Not out of any skill or luck. No, it was because I wasn't smart enough to dodge. I'd stand there and not move, as my cousin would sit behind me and light and load the bottle rockets. The first one to move lost. I wasn't smart enough to move.

Time rolled on and the only change was from elementary school to junior high school, in the nearest "town" (Not much of a town, but it was all we had, with 3,500 people.) It was two years of drab uncertainty. I went to school and suffered through all the usual pubescent horrors. I don't remember much about it. Just that it was there, and I was there.

In between my seventh and eighth grade school years, I grew seven inches, and besides stressing my parents' already-lean school clothes budget, it made me the tallest kid in my class. That, along with my reputation as an outsider, made me a target. Again.

I remember standing, for some damned reason, in the stairwell of our depression-era junior high school, when a self-styled badass came by. He looked at me, and just hauled off and punched me. I remember being totally surprised at the punch, but I also remember that I was shocked by the fact that it rocked my head but didn't do anything else. I was raised on television, and when *Mannix* or *Peter Gunn* or Kookie from *77 Sunset Strip* punched someone, they went down, or slammed into a wall. I just stood there, surprised, because I didn't even know the guy. He left and avoided me the rest of the school year.

Now, that sounds like I'm thinking I'm some kind of badass. I'm not. But I think he was also surprised that nothing happened, and figured he'd made whatever stupid point he intended to make.

I was thinking about that punch later, at home, thinking that I was a target for physical threats, which was quite an escalation from the years of insults I'd endured because I was different. I was getting used to that.

5

While in junior high school, I discovered the local library, the Scenic Regional Library. I don't know what was so scenic about it. It was downtown, about ten blocks or so from the junior high. Once a month I could walk down there after school and my dad would pick me up on his way home from work. I always had a load of books, often five or more. Each month, rain or shine or snow or sleet or stinging sun, I made that walk with a stack of books and spent an hour leafing through the shelves and finding more treasures.

I read war stories and science fiction and science nonfiction. I'd fill out dozens of order cards for books. When one came in, it was almost like Christmas.

I used to think that this fixation with the library was the product of a geek not fitting in and finding a place to hide. I don't think that anymore. Remember those horizons? They weren't just physical. I was starting into the years of my dissatisfaction, I think. When you're twelve, you can't just ship out and go see what's out there. But my mind would go and go and go and go. I mined diamonds on Venus with Norton, caught a huge fish with Hemingway, slogged through the jungles with Tregaskis, and caught criminals with Gardner. I soared through space with Heinlein, dove with Cousteau, and gunned down the bad guy with L'Amour.

And, then I'd go back to the school, and do my chores, and, and, and . . .

I started fishing about that time, too. Not because I just love to fish. It was the one time where people expected you to sit down and be quiet, and it was some kind of sin to move or talk, "Because the fish could hear you." I didn't care what I caught. I didn't care *if* I caught anything. I just had the time to spend looking at things and thinking about them. Junior high was, until recently, the most in-touch with myself that I'd been. I was comfortable with myself.

I remember being at my grandpa's pond, sitting there and thinking that I wasn't so smart, or I would have all this figured out. You know, life, and why I was different. I had the reputation that I was a nerdy brain in school. I realized that it wasn't that I was so smart, it's just that I *thought*. I realized then that many people just didn't think. Not about why they did things or why they were the way they were. They just were . . . there. They kind of filled a slot but didn't do anything else.

It was kind of heady. I was inordinately proud of my insight. A kind of internal self-congratulation.

This habit of thinking deeply about things was one of the reasons my oldest cousin and I were so close. Imagine two boys, probably eleven or twelve years old, sitting in the middle of a couple hundred acres of cattle pastureland or on the bank of a stock pond, wearing nothing but cutoff jeans. Those boys aren't discussing cows or farming or school. Those boys are discussing time travel paradoxes and the latest breakthroughs in physics or the state of the space program. We were different. We continue to be different.

We marched to a drum that only we could hear, although both of us marched to a different tune. One night at dinner, my cousin remarked that we never got involved in gangs or succumbed to peer pressure, because we were born into a gang. We were the Hoppe Boys. What others thought, or what they felt we should become, didn't matter to us a bit. We developed and lived by our own code of honor and integrity. Although morals are a slippery thing, our own unwritten code of conduct was immovable, and always present.

6

If junior high school was the start of looking beyond the horizons, then high school was the start of an awakening. The awakening of a personality. The eggshell was breaking, but this was no passive *cheep, cheep, cheep*. This was the raucous birth of a tornado and the shattering explosion of Mount St. Helens, but all happening in silence, because I knew that, if I let out what was inside of me, I would be branded, again, as *different*. Above all, teenage boys don't want to be *different*.

This was the time when I tried things that were bold and daring, and even dangerous. Nope, not what you're thinking. As a matter of fact, I wasn't into breaking the law—yet. I never used drugs. My first taste of beer (other than sipping the god-awful stuff that my dad and his friends drank) was after helping decorate for my senior prom. No, I just started to express myself, and to look inward. For that, I blame/ credit/thank Coach Sandoval.

During my junior year, a teacher showed up and broke the string of uptight white teachers. I guess he was probably Filipino, but I never asked. He came in and became the coach for our new wrestling team, and also became our philosophy teacher. But my philosophy was, to say the least, unformed. I kind of pinballed around life with no direction, just knowing that I was going . . . somewhere. And then there was Rich Sandoval. During class, held in the cafeteria because of a lack of classroom space, he would be teaching, then a female teacher would walk through, and Rich would make some schmoozing remark, like, "Hey, looking good, Miss Whatever!" Miss Whatever would blush and smile, and he would turn back to teaching like there was never an interruption. He would say things that our neo-Baptist, uptight, "What will the neighbors think?" world just didn't allow. Not only would he say or do those things, but people liked it. I realized the first time I saw it happen that there was value in being exactly who you are and not giving a shit what others thought.

He taught philosophy in class and life lessons during wrestling practice. He adopted all of us, in a way, especially those of us who were looking at far horizons. He had been places, done things, and always, always, went his own way. He was a rebel in a time and place where rebels weren't wanted, and he made it look oh-so cool. I looked up to this guy so much. I realized that I needed to go my own way, find a new path, whatever metaphor you want to use, because I wanted to be cool, like Coach.

I found out that the only thing waiting at the end of a rebel's path is the life lesson that you can't fake *cool*. You have to earn it, and if you try and fail, it's a hard, hard road through life.

I played football and wrestled. I don't know exactly why, but I remember thinking that it was expected. I was good enough, but you'd have to really care about it, and I didn't. Not really. Our sports teams sucked pretty badly, and I couldn't understand the kids who were shattered because the football team lost or because the basketball team finished at the bottom of the district. It happened often enough; I remember thinking that we should just be used to it.

7

I had my first girlfriend. I didn't really blame her when she dumped me. I was different. She didn't want different. I was finding out that nobody did.

I had my second girlfriend. Well, in my mind, she was a girlfriend. In her mind, I imagine the characterization of our relationship was somewhat different. You see, I was different. She didn't want different. She wanted my cousin. The night that I realized it, we'd gone to the pizza place (Pizza Shack! Hamburger, green pepper, and onion pizza, with an orange soda to wash it down!) and ran into my cousin and one of his friends there. I realized the look she gave him, and the way that she brightened up when he was near. When I took her home, I was proud of myself. She opened the door and started to get out and I said, "I don't think we'll do this again. If you want something, don't use someone else to get it." I reached across, pulled the door shut, and left.

All through high school, I had a few girlfriends. Frankly, I dated them because I just wanted to belong somewhere, not because I wanted to belong with *them*. There were a few who were different, who were girl (hyphen) friends, as opposed to girlfriends.

Then there were the crushes, and tragic damsels, not the least of whom was Betty. Betty wasn't any beauty. She was cute or attractive or whatever you called that, but most importantly, she was considered part of the in-crowd. Just in case I have to say this . . . I wasn't—part of the in-crowd, that is.

I was walking from one school building to another one afternoon, in between classes, and I was going to my car, when I saw Betty sitting on the tailgate of the truck that she drove. Just sitting there, looking down, not moving.

Something about her pose and demeanor bothered me. I stopped and stood there for a few seconds or minutes, and finally asked her if she was alright.

Let me back up.

My oldest sister had a couple of close friends, one of whom was Charlie. I vaguely recall that she had long strawberry blond hair. Anyway, Charlie, my sister, and Betty's older sister, Beverly, usually hung out together. Beverly had this Jeep. One night, when Beverly and Charlie were out, as I heard the story, they were driving with the top off the Jeep, going through town. It was a little brisk, so they had a blanket. The blanket started to blow out, and Charlie kind of stood to retrieve it. Just then, Beverly hit a bump in the street. Charlie came out at about forty miles an hour and died on impact with the ground. She was seventeen. This was a shattering occurrence in a town of 3,500. Beverly never quite got over it. The feeling of guilt, I mean. She was never the same again. As a matter of fact, I don't recall that I ever saw her smile again.

So, when I asked Betty what was wrong, she looked up. She had been crying and looked like hell, and said, "Beverly."

I stopped and sat down with her. We sat there for I don't know how long. Just sat. We didn't talk. At all. Just sat.

Soon, she stopped crying. She pulled a handkerchief out of her purse, wiped her tears, blew her nose, then looked at me. I just looked back.

She said, "Thank you."

And we went our separate ways.

I fell really heavily for a girl during the beginning of my senior year. I was head over heels for her. It was all about her. I couldn't wait to see her, and we spent every possible moment together, and I was incredibly in love. Well, what passes for love in high school, anyway. We couldn't hardly talk about anything important, and she was terrible for me. We could barely stand to be around each other more than an hour or two at a time, it seemed, but we craved to be with each other. She was a bad girl, and I was warned away from her. Of course, I was smart, so I knew better, and I stayed with her.

She was a resident at a children's home, taken away from her father after they discovered he'd been molesting her for years.

When I found out that she had been engaged all this time to some guy in St. Louis, and that I was just convenient while she was going to school, well, I was more than shattered. It was like a huge pillow had dropped over me, and everything around me was muffled and I was numb.

She told me over the phone. Then she asked me what I was going to do. I said something like "I'm going to do whatever I feel like." She said, and this still mystifies me, "You don't have the guts to kill yourself." I opened my mouth to tell her that killing myself had never entered my mind, and then just shut it. I slowly hung up the phone.

I got in my car and drove to Chicago. I don't know why I did. I don't remember the trip, either. I just remember looking out over the lake as the sun was coming up behind me.

I learned a lesson. Bad girls are bad. That's why they're called that. I've never forgotten that. It's not that I never dated another bad girl. It's just that I never expected them to be more than they are.

8

The next mold for me to break was drugs—or actually, not doing drugs.

I was working at the warehouse at the amusement park, Six Flags Over Mid-America. The warehouse crews were kind of the elite of the seasonal workers there. You had to be male, you had to be over six feet tall, and you had to be used to doing manual labor. We also wore these chambray work shirts and Levi's jeans and work boots. The other male employees had to wear these fruity, *look at me, I'm a lollipop on acid* uniforms. We looked masculine. They looked like tea cozies.

Even in those days, I was an outsider. I didn't go for the strutting and preening that the rest of the crew did. But let's just say I dated a lot. Six Flags was the date factory to end all date factories. There was a LOT of sex going on. I'd been dating a girl, Terri, who was Daddy's little girl, and she loved sex. Beautiful and brainless. And she was boring the hell out of me. No conversation, no laughter. I'd pick her up, we'd fondle each other on the way to wherever we were going. I'd endure her stupid laugh, and then we'd go somewhere and screw. It was stupefyingly boring, and I needed a change from the *hop from one cheerleader to another* thing I had going on.

One day I was near the amusement park's medical clinic when I saw Pam, a non-cheerleader I'd dated a couple times. I walked up and said hi. We dated—well, mauled—each other a few times, and hadn't parted on bad terms, so I figured we'd just talk. Well, we talked for a while, and then she said, "I just have to ask your name!" Man, I was crushed. We'd had a real hot thing going, and it had just been three months since I'd last seen her. I said, "Pam, it's me! Rick!" And she laughed, and told me that she wasn't Pam. She noticed the confused, stupid look on my face, and not knowing me well enough to know that it was my standard look, she told me that she was Pam's twin sister, Samantha. Get it? Pam and Sam. After about a half hour, I was finally convinced that she was, indeed, Pam's twin. Seems that they were separated in grade school when their parents divorced. Pam went to live with their mother, and Sam went to live with her father in Chicago. Well, it seems that Daddy was gone all the time, so Sam came to live with her sister and mother, and there we found ourselves. Well, if Pam was a free spirit, Sam was WILD! A one-hour conversation with her left you winded and spinning. So, we started dating. That's when we get to the drug thing.

Another thing about Six Flags is that there was always a party. Usually, they started in the picnic area about a half hour after the park closed and went till the sun came up. I took Sam to one of these parties, and about 3 a.m., we were all sitting around in a circle and talking. I didn't drink much in those days, if ever. But the joints started passing around the circle. When it got to me, I passed it on to the next person. I didn't smoke, but I didn't care if anyone else did. There was a guy next to me who was working real, real hard to get into Sam's pants. Sam had been hanging on my arm most of the night, and we'd been kind of pawing each other. I passed the joint to this guy, who by the way was named Guy, and he said, "What's your problem, jock-o? Scared?" So, I hit him. Hard. Right hand, clean across the body in a looping punch, dead on the old nose. It squashed like a bug, blood all over the place, and he started screaming. I mean, his nose was laying off to the side, streaming blood. So, I grabbed him and applied a technique I'd learned during my wrestling days. I've broken my nose a lot and I've found it to be much less painful to set it myself than to wait until a doctor can get to it, so I popped his nose back into place. If you've ever done that, well, you know it hurts, probably more than the original break did. That and it's noisy. Like the world's biggest Rice Krispie. Snap, Crackle, Pop, nose reset. I turned to ask Sam if she wanted to leave and she yelled, "What's your fucking problem?" I said, and I'll remember this till the day I die, "The problem is that I have the wrong friends." And I got up and left. I don't know how Sam got home. And I didn't care.

I never spoke to her again.

And I never tried drugs, just to be stubborn, but also because, while stoners outwardly appear to be accepting and mellow and nonjudgmental, for me, they were just one more pressure group where you had to conform to be accepted. And I never conformed. I already knew, at seventeen, that I was different. How could I be otherwise?

When I was working at Six Flags, I met a woman who was definitely the opposite of the cheerleader type. Her name was Eileen. She was pretty but not beautiful. Pleasantly shaped but not sexy. However, she entranced me with our conversations. She worked at one of the many ice-cream stands in the park, and I'd met her as I was delivering ice cream to her. Eventually, and for the life of me I don't remember how, we ended up going out. It was one of those *night shift* dates. I was working the night shift at the warehouse and had to be at work by 6 p.m. I picked her up mid-morning and we went out to eat somewhere. Then we went by her house. And I met her sister. Eileen's sister was a Down syndrome child. I didn't know what that meant, and wouldn't hear the label for many years, but she was just like other Down syndrome kids that I've met. Loving, kind, happy, and fiercely loved by her family.

And I never went out with Eileen again.

I don't know why. I don't *think* it was because of her sister. I'm *pretty sure* it wasn't because of her sister. But Eileen probably thought that it was. And I'd give anything to meet her again and tell her that I was no great catch of a human being, and that I'm sorry if I hurt her.

And here, I have to talk about J. She doesn't know to this day how I felt, or how I think I felt about her.

This is complicated.

Alright, I've talked at least a bit about being in my cousin's shadow. It was a fact of life, but I was chafing at the bit about it. I was ready to be me, to be Rick. Whoever in the hell that happened to be. But, while I lived in that little town, I was *his* cousin. Oh, yeah, he also happened to have a name. But before you get the feeling that my cousin was some kind of ogre or something—well, he wasn't, and isn't to this day—I must admit, he just had it all.

You know. The *it* that society wants you to have all of. Looks. Brains. Athletic ability. Natural musculature. *It!* I, on the other hand, hardly had any of *it*. So, I ran into way too many women who wanted to get next to him and didn't have any problem using me to get there. Women who I would be interested in and who couldn't see me because they spent all their time looking for *him*. If I did well in a class, *he* did better. If I won a wrestling match, *he* won the football game.

By the time I was a senior, I pretty much resented him. You know exactly what I'm talking about. That immature, post-adolescent resentment. That *this doesn't make any sense and I want to be mad at someone so it might as well be my friend who I love* kind of resentment. I don't remember exactly when, and I don't remember exactly how, but there was J. She just came into my life. Somehow. I don't remember. She arrived like the dawn. Slowly, I guess, starting as a glimmer, then a glow, then the all-encompassing light.

J was in love with my cousin, but she was my friend.

I don't know how it happened, but she turned out to be my best friend. We talked about everything. EVERYTHING! Spell the letters out separately, *E-V-E-R-Y-T-H-I-N-G!* Unfortunately, she often wanted to talk about my cousin. Not raving about how great he was, but *what the hell was his problem* and *why couldn't he see her?*

I wasn't any help there. I *could* see her. All too well. I liked to think that I was in love with her, but I wasn't. She was my friend. I think that's it. You know how I know I loved her, but I wasn't *in love* with her? She was beautiful and hot. She could melt me with the way she wore her jeans and her smile and her eyes. The only woman I ever knew who would crinkle her nose when she laughed, and it wasn't a cutesy act.

I never tried to seduce her. I don't even think I ever kissed her. I don't even think it crossed my mind. I had all the correct parts; I had all the required teenage hormones. But she was my friend, and my best friend, and she filled my soul with her friendship. I never, ever felt the need to prove I was a man. I had this sense of honor—that *thank God* survives (somewhat) to this day—and I couldn't have tried to *make a move* on her, because she wasn't mine. If she was anyone's, she was my cousin's. And that was cool, because I was filled with my first real friendship with a woman.

Even though there was nothing sexual between us, she never failed to make me feel like a man. She'd put her arm around my waist (yes, I had one in those days), and hug me close, and I felt like the biggest, tallest, strongest, happiest man in the world.

She was my first. First girl . . . friend. First best friend. My first introduction into the world of mature emotion. I don't know what would have happened had we continued.

I never got to find out.

A couple days after graduation from high school, her sister told me that she'd left, to go to Arkansas, I think.

Not a word. No goodbye.

It was a wonder. I was crushed, but it was strange. I trusted her. She had a reason for it.

But I couldn't help but feeling lost and forgotten. It was a feeling that I would grow to know like an old friend.

9

Graduation happened. That's it. It happened. It wasn't this huge event; it wasn't the grand culmination of twelve years of work. It happened. I remember it not for the triumph but for the embarrassment.

After the graduation ceremony, my cousin and I went driving around. There was a huge graduation party by the river, and we'd heard that the county sheriff knew about it and was going to bust it. So, we went to the truck stop and drank coffee, then started driving around. We graduated in 1974, so when we passed mile marker 74 on Interstate 44, it just seemed right to take it.

A couple hours later, I was standing on a guardrail taking down another one. When the cop pulled up, we dropped down and looked for a way out, but our car was sitting there, so we were busted. We had thirteen signs in the car.

He talked about arresting us for petty larceny and possession of burglary tools. Then he started adding up the costs of signs, and the next thing you know, we were only charged with petty larceny.

Six months of probation and a $100 fine. And endless embarrassment.

10

I tried college. It wasn't for me. I knew that. It was boring. BORING!!! I wanted to learn great things, fantastic things, things that would opened my world. And what I learned was that I didn't want to be there. And, as always, I was in my cousin's shadow there too. Here's the problem with that. You know who put me in that shadow? Me! Just me! Shit, I hope one day I can find the courage to apologize to my cousin for what I thought and what I felt.

I felt the pull of the road, or the world, or something. I knew it was something. My oldest sister was living in St. Louis and doing work that made me realize that most people do boring jobs for idiots, and they start to die when they go to work.

I knew I couldn't do that. I couldn't do it. But what options did I have?

I'd set my feet on a road, and I didn't know where it was going. I know that now. But the sense of unease—the sense of being out of place—was growing. I limped through a year of college. A year that I was less than mediocre at. Except for the opposite sex, dating, getting laid thing. That went extremely well. And really, really, poorly.

I found out that sex didn't mean a damn thing without some level of personal attraction. It was a pretty heady realization for an eighteen-year-old, and one that I learned to keep to myself. If my brain isn't engaged, nothing else was going to work right. Or work at all. I worried about it for a bit, then realized what was happening, and I was good with it.

It wasn't that I didn't care about college, but even then, I had a sense that I wasn't where I was supposed to be. I'd borrowed a line from *Support Your Local Sheriff*, the 1969 Western movie with James Garner. I'd tell people, "Basically, I'm on my way to Australia." I knew even then that I, in my mind, could substitute "Australia" for *I'm going somewhere, and it won't be here.*

The next year passed, and I sank deeper and deeper into the small-town quicksand, but there were flashes of what was to come.

I met a woman at college, and I was smitten from the start. I don't remember her name, but I met her in the cafeteria. I was standing at the coffee pot, and the song "Piano Man" came on. She was standing behind me, and I turned to her and asked if she knew who that was. The reason that I asked was that he sounded amazingly like Harry Chapin, who I'd just started getting into that year. She told me it was Billy Joel, and that he was inspired by Harry Chapin. She got her coffee, and we went to a table and talked for hours. It probably wasn't that long, but we closed the cafeteria. She was olive-skinned and her hair was frizzy, never styled. She wore work shirts or flannel shirts and corduroy pants. She didn't have a good figure, and she wasn't the least bit interested in playing the coy female, wasn't interested in the dating game. So, of course we started dating, or kind of dating—or hell, I don't know what to call it. We'd go to a diner or a restaurant and sit and talk. We'd stand outside the house where she was staying and talk until dawn. I never touched her, not even a hug. I don't remember her name.

If I'd been farther along the road, we would have been great friends.

Somehow, we, probably I, drifted apart.

The world wasn't done emphasizing how little I had in common with *normal*.

One night, a friend and I were leaving the Pizza Shack, and I saw a friend of mine, Dianne, in a car with her boyfriend. I don't know where he was from, and don't remember his name, but I do remember that none of us liked him. He was greasy and argumentative. Anyway, he and Dianne were arguing rather loudly, and I saw him draw back his hand and slap her. I yelled at him and started to walk to the car. He started to open the door, and Dianne yelled, "He's got a gun! RUN!"

And time slowed down.

He had one leg outside of the car, and I launched against the door and heard his leg break, this horrendous, echoing, wet, slapping snap. He howled, Dianne screamed, the gun came flying out of the car, and my friend (I don't remember his name) grabbed me and started dragging me to my car. I went.

I ran into Dianne a couple of months later. She was furious with me. She said that my actions caused the guy to break up with her.

I was mystified because I thought that was kind of the point.

To this day, I still don't understand. I understand, though, that I felt nothing—no remorse, no regret. Nothing. It was a little taste of my future.

What was significant about this incident was that I instantly went from concern to applied violence in defense of someone, without a thought or hesitation. I was a little disturbed by that, but I didn't realize that it would become kind of a *thing* for me in years to come.

11

I t wasn't all teenage drama, though. There were things that made me sit up and notice how the world worked, things that made me grow emotionally.

I worked at a convenience store. I don't remember why I was working there instead of Six Flags. It might have been that they didn't want me back. It might have been that I didn't want to go back. I just don't know. Anyway, I found out that I was pretty good with people when I wanted to be.

There was a guy, probably in his fifties, who came in darn near every day after he got off work. He would walk in the door and say, "How ya doin'?" and head for the beer cooler. He'd get a six-pack of Stag beer. (You haven't tasted bad beer till you've tasted Stag. Or Falstaff.) Then I'd put it into a small sack, sideways so he could take beers out as he drove.

There was a married woman who would come in, and even though I knew she was married, I was still a rather large bundle of hormones. She was twenty-eight. I was eighteen. She was tall and willowy with red hair and green eyes. She always wore these big sunglasses. We'd talk, and I'd make passes at her, suggesting that we go play tennis or see a movie. One day, she walked in wearing the sunglasses and I asked her name. She told me, and I realized that she was married to one of the guys who was known as a badass in town. The town had a population of 3,500 people, so you can imagine the slime who got to be known as a badass. That somehow made it more exciting. Yeah, I know. There's a fine line between brave and stupid, and in this, I was way over that line.

The next time she came up to the counter, I asked her to take off her sunglasses. She pulled them down to show me not only the most marvelous green eyes but also a week-old, purple, yellow, and black bruising eye.

I didn't know what to say. She got this embarrassed look in her eyes, and before she could pull the glasses up, I said, "Beautiful eyes." She paid and hurried out the door. I figured that was the last I'd see of her.

She used to come in only once or twice a week, but she drove into the parking lot the next day and sat in her car for about half an hour. I was getting concerned, so I walked out and asked her if she was alright. She said she didn't know if she should get out of the car or not.

Call me Captain Oblivious. I told her that was up to her, but I'd sure like it if she did. I went back inside, and she drove off. She showed up sometime after 10 p.m., when I'd closed the store. I walked over and told her that the store was closed. She just looked at me. I stood there. Then I got in her car.

We—oh, I don't know what you call it—dated, I guess, from June until I joined the Army in August. No commitment. No recriminations. No remorse on my part. I found her beautiful and tragic. I think she found me horny and available. Oh, don't forget, "easy." It was okay. I was drawn by the tragedy of her. She had been popular in high school, was a college graduate, and then for some reason decided to marry the bad boy and spend her life trying to escape him emotionally but being bound to him physically. I couldn't understand that dynamic at the time, and I still don't understand. My worldview has a very direct approach to someone who tries to hurt me. I hurt 'em right back. Of course, at 6'3" and 300 pounds, I have a much better chance at getting away with that than a 5'7" woman who weighs in at 140 pounds or so.

The day I joined the Army, I told her that same night. She had come to the store to see me after closing, so we were sitting in her car. After I shut the door, she noticed that something was different, and asked "What's going on?" I told her that I was leaving in a few days for basic training. She looked at me, long and deeply, leaned over, kissed me, then reached past me to open the door. I got out of the car, and she drove away. No words. Not a backwards look. I respected that.

I don't remember her name. Funny. I can remember the color of her shirt the first time she let me undress her, and that she wore size 8.5 shoes, but I don't remember her name. There's a conclusion to be drawn there, but I'll be damned if I know what it is.

Then, there was G. I have to mention G. She was a friend of my older sister, so she would have been about twenty-two or twenty-three when I knew her. Fairly often, she and I would work a shift at the store together. I found her pixie-ish, and cute. Upturned nose, a light dusting of freckles, and of course, I made passes at her. But mostly, we talked.

G married a hometown boy but yearned to travel and see new things, and I fantasized about finding someone like her. But hometown boy was a beer-drinkin', hell-raisin', river-fishin', softball-playin' kind of guy. His idea of a great vacation was going to St. Louis to see the Cardinals play, or going to the Lake of the Ozarks, or drinking beer and hootin' and hollerin' at all the tourists.

One Friday night G's husband had the car and didn't come get her when we closed the store. I couldn't leave her alone at the store, so after an hour and a half, I gave her a ride home.

Keep in mind that my making passes at G was reflex. In reality, I liked her a lot, but that was it.

So, we get to her house, a trailer, of course, and the front door is open, but the car is gone. I go in with her to make sure that there's not a burglar or something. The house is a wreck, with beer cans and bottles all over the place. There's a note on the table, barely legible, saying that hubby-boy is going to the Lake of the Ozarks with his buddies for the weekend. She just stood there, and her shoulders slumped. I put my hand on her shoulder and asked her if she wanted me to call her sister or something. She turned, grabbed my hand, and pulled me back toward the bedroom.

There wasn't a word said in that moment.

Not a word.

I learned that night that there's a huge difference between lovemaking and sex.

No frenzy. No adolescent angst. Two candles. Two people.

And I knew it wasn't because she was in love with me. I knew why she did it, why we did that.

I knew, and my mind was spinning, literally spinning, with the realization that she had been humiliated, neglected, put in second place, belittled, and ignored. She needed to feel like a woman, needed to feel in charge of something. She was such a gentle soul; it was a pleasure and a joy and even an honor to be there for her. To give her no demands and to let her dictate our actions and our pace. To cool down, sweat drying, smiling, and talking till dawn. I got in my car and left, her standing on the porch in her robe, waving and crying and smiling.

I was in a whirl. I didn't have a conquest. I wasn't in love with her. She wasn't in love with me. Because I only had one week before I left for basic training, I would probably never see her again, and it was okay.

A few months later, my mom told me she ran into G at the grocery store. G had moved in with her sister after filing for a divorce, and she was smiling and happy. I don't know that I had anything to do with that, but I hope that I did.

G died of lymphatic, breast, and lung cancer on August 12, 1998, at the age of forty-seven.

I'd like to put one of those terse little endings on this scene, but I won't. What I'd like you to do is see a little button nose, freckles, blue, blue, sky-blue eyes, and a smile that could light up two people's faces. That's what I see. I'm smiling now.

12

So, from outsider geeky kid to the Romeo of the convenience stores, but you have to wonder, how did I end up in the Army? I'm actually not quite sure *why* I ended up in the Army, but here's how it went.

August 19, 1975, I'm sleeping in my bed, in my basement room in my parents' house. It's sunny outside, and the house is dead quiet. My parents and three sisters are in Florida on vacation. I don't know why I didn't go, but I know that I wasn't upset about being left behind, so it was probably my choice to stay home. I sat up in bed, and said, "I guess I'll go join the Army." I tell people this and they figure that I'm leaving something out, that it doesn't happen that way, but it did.

No . . . prior . . . thought . . . whatsoever.

That simple. I don't know why I did it. I wasn't on the run from the law. No judge had told me that it was the Army or the county jail. I had a good job and was going to college, I was meeting women, and overall, life was good. And I hated it with a passion.

I can't tell you, for sure, why I hated it, but I did. Something about a small town not being big enough maybe. I don't know, and at this late date, it just doesn't matter. I know that it wasn't my parents, my sisters, or anything about living at home. We weren't really poor, but there was never much extra money for things. We never noticed it. We had the woods to run in, the pond to fish in. My parents were loving and not mean or brutal or abusive. I just never fit in. I wasn't a geek. I was big and strong. I was an athlete who devoured books like some kids devour hamburgers. I always had a girlfriend or two. I was working at a convenience store, and that led me to discover the joys of older women. But I hated my life, or more correctly, I hated where it wasn't going.

So, by 11:00 a.m., I was in a recruiter's office in the county seat. He looked up and said, "Can I help you?" And I replied, "I want to join the Army." I remember the surprised look on his face. Now I know that it was because this was the very, very beginning of the all-volunteer Army. The draft ended the previous year, and I had a draft lottery number and a draft card, but no one was getting drafted. I vaguely recall seeing reports about the final and embarrassing fall of Vietnam, and nothing else was going on. Now, recruiters were the only way that anyone was joining the Army, and the reputation of the post-Vietnam (post-Mỹ Lai) Army was in shreds. And here comes this kid, saying, "I want to join the Army."

The following afternoon, after the required poking and prodding and testing, I was sworn into the Army on delayed entry. I was on delayed entry because I figured I should wait till my parents came home so they could say goodbye. I also had surprised the recruiter a second time. I'd scored in the top 5 percent in my entry tests, which meant I could probably choose any field I wanted, but I still wanted to be an infantryman.

That night, I called my parents in their hotel room in Florida and blandly told them that I joined the Army. I remember a long pause on the other end of the phone, and my mother saying, "Mel (my dad), you need to talk to him." I thought that was because joining the Army was a male bonding thing, that my dad would be proud. Now I know it was because Mom wanted Dad to talk me out of it or something. He didn't try, and I wouldn't have listened.

A week later, my parents and I were at the truck stop up the road from the house at 4:15 a.m. to meet the recruiter. We said goodbye.

I'd crossed a border and could never look back on the same land again.

Rick's Rules of Life number eighteen is "You CAN go home again. It just won't be there."

It's not that anything about my home had changed. That was the problem with staying. Nothing ever changed. No, the change was internal, and affected my vision as I looked back, forever turning green summers and ice-blue winters into black-and-white snapshots.

I wanted different, and oh my God, basic and advanced training was different. The physical part wasn't a problem. I was a wrestler, and even through the summer, I kept my conditioning up. I benched over 300 pounds for a workout, squatted over 400 pounds, and could run all day. The only problem was I had about 3 percent body fat, so I had to eat like a horse in order to fuel the machine.

My awareness of my physical condition (and my damned ego!) led to some . . . interesting interactions with the drill sergeants. You want pushups? I'll push until the audience gets tired. You want me to carry heavy loads for long distances? No problem, I'll hump gear like a star mule, all day long. You want me to give due respect to people who maybe don't have my level of condition and fitness? Well, that was a problem. Actually, it started to be a problem, but the drill sergeants "fixed" it.

I remember that I was scoffing at the physical conditioning of my fellow trainees when I caught the attention of Drill Sergeant Robinson.

Sergeant First Class Robinson was an impressive specimen of a soldier. He wasn't muscled up. He was quiet and pretty reserved. He sometimes called cadence but mostly just walked around, ensuring that our training was being done to standard, and every once in a while, he found something that required his personal attention. One day, that *something* was me and my attitude. Yeah, I know, if you know me, you are shocked, shocked, I tell you, that I had an attitude.

Drill Sergeant Robinson was educating me on the importance of respecting my fellow unit members. He was doing so by having me do enough pushups to *make him tired*. He wasn't getting tired. Not fast enough, anyway. But I was not having much of a problem doing pushups. So, Drill Sergeant Robinson felt that he needed to be a bit more direct. He squatted down by my head and said, "So, babycakes [yeah, they actually talked that way], you think you are so much better than they are?" I was dumb, but not dumb enough to answer that one in any other way than by saying, "No, Drill Sergeant!" Drill Sergeant Robinson leaned forward and whispered in my ear, "Bullshit!" Then he hauled off and punched me in the side of the head, and I found myself face down in the gravel, wondering what the fuck had just happened. My eyes were kind of rolling around, and the stars that were dancing in my head were really pretty, and I heard Drill Sergeant Robinson's voice whisper, "It's not so fucking funny now, is it?"

I tried to agree, but my voice wasn't connected to my brain, so I just moaned.

I can't tell you much about the training. I remember snapshots of marching, the haircuts, and the bull sessions in the barracks. There are a couple of things, though, that stuck in my mind.

The first one happens in the context of my upbringing and exposure to other races. Specifically, to Black people. I was ignorant of any other cultures or beliefs. There were two Black families in our town. That was it. We played football together, we hung out together, and I didn't think much of it. Except for their skin color, they were just, well, they were just kids, like me.

One Sunday, during morning inspection, the drill sergeant asked if anyone wanted to go to a church service off-post. Hell, I jumped at the chance. I think I was getting a little stir-crazy, a little barracks fever. So, they piled us into a van, I think. When we got there, I realized that I was in for a new experience.

If you've never attended a Full Gospel, Black Baptist church service, well, I can tell you that you are missing something wonderful. We pulled up, and there was me and one other white kid, and everyone else was Black. And they were wonderful! They greeted us and put us in a pew in the front row, and they were all dressed up in their finest Sunday wear. I was probably looking around, appearing lost, but all I saw were smiles. And then the fun began. The preacher began, kind of like that Neil Diamond song, "Brother Love's Travelling Salvation Show" with the lyrics "like a small earthquake. And when he lets go, half the valley shakes!"

I wasn't religious. I was raised Methodist, but not devout, and I hadn't been to church in years. My parents tried, but it never took. So, this preacher let go, and I'd never heard anything like that! He was sweating and shouting, and then the ladies of the church started getting happy. They'd stand and start dancing in place, and I wondered what the heck was going on. They'd be so euphoric that they'd start to fall over and their neighbors in the pews would hold them up, and the rest of the service was a blur. What kind of state would cause people to do that? What was the point? What the preacher was saying was fine. I'd heard all that before, but never with that much energy, never with that much passion. But, these folks, Black folks living in rural south Louisiana, well, they were happy and loving and giving and passionate, right along with the preacher. Then it was over. I felt like I was floating on a cloud. My mind was stretched out to receive these new images, and these ladies grabbed me and told me that I had to come to lunch with them. So I did.

I was concerned that these wonderful people would have little to share, so I was relieved when I saw that there was plenty of food. The tables were groaning with food like I had never-before eaten— juicy ham hocks, slabs of ham a half-inch thick, cornbread so light you could barely keep it on your plate, three or four different kinds of greens, sweet potatoes, which we only got on Thanksgiving. Then there were the pies and cobblers and puddings and cakes. All of it was very simple, but it was delicious and there was so much of it. I ate until I couldn't eat anymore and then ate two slices of something

I'd never known existed—sweet potato pie, a food of the gods! By the time I left, I was hugged by every woman in the place, had my hand shaken by every man. I'd been smiling so much my cheeks hurt. And I'd been kissed on the cheek by every grandmother in the place.

Sounds pretty dynamite, huh?

Then why was I so blue the next week? I know now why. I'd gotten a whole lot of my preconceptions and, yes, even prejudices, blasted out of the sky, and was beginning to wonder what else I'd accepted as true that wasn't. It's not that my family was taught to hate Black people. But most of the older members of my family and many people who lived in our area of rural Missouri were products of their upbringing and environment. I accepted their attitudes out of ignorance.

My soul started to rotate out of its niche, and it wasn't so much painful as disorienting. It wasn't like my folks lied to me. I just thought that the world withheld things from me, things that I didn't know existed, things that I didn't know *could* exist! I wasn't depressed, but I thought that I was king of a domain, and now I realized that we are all kings, if we want to be, and I was nothing special.

I was evolving, relooking at myself and everything that I knew to be true, and made me wonder what would come next.

13

The second thing that struck tested my preconceived notion of who I was and what I valued came a few weeks into basic training.

When you go to the hand grenade range, you sit in a tunnel, and the first person in line goes forward to a grenade pit. They hand you a grenade, and you, on command, pull the pin, aim, and throw it over a wall, then hit the dirt, all while the drill sergeant hovers over you to make sure you don't catch any shrapnel.

Well, one of the guys grabbed the grenade, and then threw, hard. Straight forward. It hit the wall and bounced off and over the rear wall, then rolled down into the tunnel. I was way at the back of the line, and I heard people yelling, "GRENADE!" and I looked up. There was this roar, and then ringing silence. Then, after a couple of seconds that must have lasted a year, there was screaming. One guy was yelling, "Momma! Momma!" I now know that, when they're hit, they start calling for Momma. It's okay. I did it too. And, like an idiot who thought he was bulletproof, I ran forward, bouncing people out of the way.

What I saw was what I imagined, in my naïve way, hell to look like. The benches on either side of the tunnel were shredded into splinters, and they looked like they'd been painted red. One of the guys, I think his name was Conway, was laying on the ground, kind of rolled up against the wall, and I had a few seconds (five, ten? I don't know) to look at him. Normally, you look at someone and expect to see the right body parts in the right areas, but I couldn't put together the mess that I saw laying up against the tunnel wall. His legs were missing flesh and streaming blood with pearly white bone showing. My mind just kind of locked up, because there was something terribly wrong with him. He kind of looked like he was just laying up against the wall of the tunnel, but then there was the blood and white bone and strips of muscle just dangling from his legs, and my mind couldn't reconcile the sight from the expectation. The grenade had detonated, evidently, right under him, and all the muscles and flesh were blown off his lower legs and part of his upper thighs. And I stopped. I couldn't move. I had my share of treating cuts and puncture wounds. After all, I lived on a farm and ran the woods all my life. But this—I didn't even know where to start. I remember a drill sergeant hitting me in the chest to get me out of the way, and I staggered back to the tunnel entrance and sat there till the three guys who were wounded were medevac'ed. I don't remember anything else about that day.

Conway died on the way to the hospital.

I had to think, but I couldn't. You see, it wasn't that Conway's legs getting blown into hamburger had screwed me up. The problem was that it *didn't* screw me up. Hell, once I got over the initial shock, it didn't really bother me. Not like it did some of the guys. There were guys in the barracks who were silently staring off into distance, and a couple were even crying. A few went immediately to the company orderly room to try to get out of the Army, or at least the infantry. I was almost alone in the chow hall when we got back. I ate a huge dinner, sitting on the barracks steps, picking my teeth; then I realized that I wasn't bothered. Not bothered in the least.

The hugeness of it was blinding me like staring into the sun. I was raised in that Midwest, Methodist religious tradition. Thou shalt not kill. Thou shalt not kill. You *will not* kill. Okay, I didn't kill Conway. But... but... but... wasn't I supposed to feel something? Anything? What was previously some kind of intellectual exercise was now very, very real. I was training to kill. I was training to throw a grenade and blow some other schmuck's legs to hamburger. I know, I know, I was supposed to reevaluate my situation and try to figure out if I was able to kill and reconcile it with my upbringing. That wasn't what was bothering me. What was bothering me was the fact that it didn't bother me. What kind of animal was I? I reached deep inside and tried to find some revulsion at the idea of killing, and I probed and probed it in the same way that you can't resist running your tongue over the hole where a tooth had been pulled.

Now, I know I was being a huge drama queen, and I was screaming and thrashing around inside rather than showing any outward sign of my turmoil. But I searched for a reluctance to kill, some hesitance to pull a trigger and end a life, some sorrow at the death of a comrade, and I couldn't find it. I'd read some about serial killers and how they seemed to lack a conscience. I knew I had one. But it was strangely quiet on the subject of killing. That was a very low point in my life. I can't tell you how low it was. I wanted to talk to someone. So I asked, on Sunday, to go see the chaplain. By the time I was done, the only person I wanted to kill was the chaplain. All I wanted to do was figure it out. What I got were platitudes, doctrine, and bullshit by the load. After an hour or so, I got up and left in the middle of one of the chaplain's readings of scripture. Just left.

It was Sunday, and I needed to talk to someone. My dad had spent a combat tour in Korea, so I tried to call. You only got about an hour for everyone to use one of a bank of pay phones, and each person got like five minutes to make a call. Maybe ten minutes.

I called my home number, and it just rang. There was no one home. There was no one else to call, so, to my mind, I was left alone with a sociopath. Then the phones were shut off at 9 p.m.

Everyone else wandered away, and I sat there, alone on a bench.

Then the lights shut off.

I sat there and cried, certain that I was condemned to a lifelong fight to regain my soul.

I remember very, very little of the next three weeks. Then came graduation from basic training. I got a merit promotion at the graduation ceremony. My mind was shut down, my conscience was dead, but something kept me going. I had a flair for leadership, and it was recognized. I went that afternoon and had my new stripes sewn on my greens. We had six days between basic training and infantry training, so we were all put on a pass. I flew home. Maybe being around my home and my family and my dogs would help me find whatever part I was missing. Maybe I'd forgotten to bring it with me to basic training.

The flight was pretty upbeat. I'd been sitting next to a woman who was reading a psychology text by B.F. Skinner. I'd read that same text the previous summer, so we started talking. She was going to Washington University in St. Louis and asked me to call her. I got her phone number and gave her mine, and she kissed me on the cheek as we got off the plane. I was starting to lift, a little.

I was walking down the concourse in the St. Louis airport terminal looking for my parents. Then I heard it.

"Killer." "Murderer." "Baby killer."

Suddenly, I realized that the person was talking to me. I turned my head to my left, and there she was. I didn't know her from Adam. She was probably fifty or sixty years old, but beyond that, I don't remember anything about her looks. All I remember was her continual recitation of my supposed sins. And then something happened. My numbed psyche came to life, and I started getting angry. I stopped and turned, and so did she. She started chanting, and I found it funny at the time. Now I find it sad for her. She said, "Hey, hey, LBJ, how many kids did you kill today?" For God's sake, it was 1975, and LBJ had been out of office for seven years.

Then she spit on me, and I spit back.

She started yelling and this cop came by. He said, "Lady, you oughta be glad that he just spit on you. If you'd spit on ME, you'd be going to jail with some bruises." He looked at me and stuck his hand out and said, "Welcome home, soldier!" The woman almost ran off, and I stood there, shaking his hand, and tears started coming. The cop grabbed me, none too gently, and led me to a side door. I thought I was going to be arrested for crying in public or something. He led me to a maintenance room or something similar. He handed me his handkerchief, then lit a cigarette (yes, you could smoke pretty much anywhere in those days). He waited until I was under control, then he said, and I'll never, ever forget this, "'S okay, troop. When I got back from Vietnam, I cried for two days straight. You just don't worry 'bout that. I love ya, brother." His name was . . . well, it doesn't matter what his name was. Everyone called him Chief. And he was my angel. He hugged me and gave me my soul back. We sat there for about ten minutes and talked, and then he said, "Well, you seem fine. Let's go find your folks." We walked farther down the concourse, and I saw my dad, and when I turned to introduce them to the angel in midnight blue, he was gone.

A couple of times, I started to try to find him, to look him up and thank him. But something stopped me. I think I knew, even then, why. He'd already done his job. We really didn't have anything else to talk about.

Several years ago, I searched for Chief. He died after a long illness, in November 2002. He was survived, according to the obituary in the *St. Louis Post-Dispatch*, by six children and twelve grandchildren. I looked up his oldest, a son, who lived in Webster Groves. The ritzy, rich part of town. I sent a card, telling him what his father did for me and what he meant to me. I left off my return address, and just signed it "Troop."

This is the first time I've ever told anyone in the world other than God.

14

I was already seeing the differences between my childhood and my adult reality. Some were pretty sad, and even tragic. Some were funny, and a couple were downright hilarious.

After I got home on leave, of course, we had to have the stereotypical welcome home dinner. My mom wasn't the best cook in the world, but she was used to cooking for men who worked in the fields, so food was hearty and plentiful.

We were sitting at the table and enjoying a roast with potatoes and carrots and just chatting. My family was full of questions about my training and what was next. In the middle of it, I politely asked my mother, "Do we have any fuckin' butter?" The table got quiet. Everyone was just staring at me, horrified. Well, except for my father, the combat veteran, whose head was down and his shoulders shaking with barely suppressed laughter. After I realized what I'd said, I found it hilarious, but I felt a shift in my family's relationship with me.

Years later, my mother told me it was at that moment that she knew that I was still her son, but I was becoming someone else.

It was kind of like falling off a moving car but hitting the ground running in another direction. I was still moving, but now I was walking alone.

I returned to training. This time, it was advanced individual training to transform me from a trainee into a basic infantryman. It was a good time for me, as I became fascinated by the fact that an infantryman was not lacking in intelligence, education, or training, and is not the cannon fodder kind of person that popular opinion insists that he is. A modern infantryman progresses over the years from basic apprentice through journeyman to master in his craft. He's an expert in ballistics, applied environmental science, survival, advanced first aid, disease prevention, planning, resource management, resource allocation, civil-military relations, cultural awareness, and many other subjects. If he's any good, an infantryman is a master in the application of controlled force to achieve a specific objective. I began to take pride in learning those skills, and the psychological shock of the grenade accident in basic training grew more and more distant. Advanced training at Fort Polk, Louisiana, was utterly fascinating, mentally stimulating, and in the end, strangely satisfying. I figured I was ready. I was so wrong. Hell, I couldn't even *see* wrong from where I was. Life had hammered me a little bit, but these were love taps compared to what was to come.

In January 1976, I reported to my first unit.

15

At my first assignment at Fort Carson, Colorado, I experienced the race riots, rampant drug and alcohol abuse, and corruption that characterized all levels of the US Army in the mid-1970s. There were beer machines in the dayroom, and commands turned a blind eye to alcoholism and drug addiction, lest the beasts get restless and decide to riot.

Field exercises were a joke, but a really sad joke. We were a mechanized infantry unit, expected to ride into battle in M113-A1 armored personnel carriers, called *tracks*. However, money was so tight—because taking care of the readiness of military forces was out of fashion—we didn't have fuel to run the tracks. We would fire them up once a week, just to make sure they still ran. But when we went to the field, we walked or caught a ride in a helicopter, or helo.

There wasn't enough money for blank ammunition, so we would practice assaulting an objective yelling, "Bang, bang!" We learned our trade. . . after a fashion, but we knew we were screwed if the Soviets ever invaded Europe.

Our sergeants and squad leaders were all Vietnam veterans, and I learned a phrase that helped reconcile the fact that any 1970s wartime deployment was a suicide mission. "It don't mean nothing!" Just that. We're gonna die! It don't mean nothin'. Our crew-served weapons are down. It don't mean nothin'. Our officers were a bunch of elitist pricks who saw us only as cannon fodder, over whose dead bodies they will get their promotions and trophy wives. It don't mean nothin'.

I attended some special schools, trying to become better at my trade. I learned how far I could push myself and just what I was capable of accomplishing.

I'll never forget the Northern Warfare Training Center, located on a glacier in Alaska in February, where I learned that you ain't seen cold until you've had to use an unheated latrine in negative twenty-degree weather, and the toilet seats are stainless steel.

At Jungle Warfare School in the Canal Zone in Panama and Recondo (Reconnaissance Commando) school at Camp Red Devil, Colorado, we learned tactics, patrolling, ambushes, hasty and deliberate attacks, field hygiene, reconnaissance, use of every assigned weapon, calling for artillery fire and air support, and airmobile operations. All fun, all hard to master, and all require a lifelong commitment—no matter how long or short your life was. Day by day, school by school, I lost myself in the world of the warrior, reveling in mastery of the art of "killing people and breaking things," as it has often been called.

Whenever we came in from the field, we had to clean our weapons before we were released for the day. Our lieutenant, a West Point graduate, who liked to tell us that he didn't have anything in common with us. But he was the first to hit the beer vending machine during "weapons cleaning." It wasn't uncommon to find weapons or pieces of weapons scattered throughout the battalion area because the soldier responsible for cleaning the weapon was hammered, stoned, and/or tripping, with no idea where he was or what he was supposed to be doing.

There was no professionalism, esprit de corps or job satisfaction. There was only a bunch of guys living and working on the edges of a society that cordially hated them.

16

My time at Fort Carson wasn't all bad.

I met Park my first day in my new unit, at Fort Carson, Colorado. We were roommates, and we were outsiders. It bonded us.

I loved Park. He was a little slow at times, and goofy and bumbling and clumsy, but his heart was bigger than his home state of Tennessee. He helped me get through my breakup with Trudy, my disastrous girlfriend who liked to introduce herself as my wife, while "keeping time" with other people.

Park was taller than me; his uncoordinated legs took up about half his height. He could run forever and always had a smile on his face. I loved him from the first time I met him.

Anyway, Park and I were inseparable. By the early summer of 1976, Trudy, the eternally expanding girlfriend, wasn't around much, so I hung out with Park. We did a lot through May and June. We travelled up to the mountains to catch late snow for skiing, hiking, and rappelling. We even once decided to climb Cheyenne Mountain— you know, North American Air Defense Command (NORAD). Why we didn't realize that was a big mistake, well, I don't know. We got detained by Air Force Security Police at the top, and our commander had to come get us out of the lockup. But we made it to the top.

We talked about everything during bull sessions in the barracks and watched each other's backs. In those days, the Army wasn't all one big happy family.

I told Park things I've never told anyone else. He was my brother, and I didn't know how much I had missed by not having a brother. He decided that I was going to go with him to Tennessee on leave in October when he went to attend his high school's homecoming game. He'd already decided that I was going to take his sister to the game and the dance and told me that it wouldn't bother him "a-tall" if she and I were to hit it off and get married. I told him to back away, and that I wasn't any great catch. I told him we'd talk about it later.

I don't want you to think that my life has been all tragedy, all thunder and lightning and hellfire and blood. Everything gone to hell. It wasn't.

There were funny things, interesting things.

Park and I learned to ski. Well, that wasn't really true. I learned to ski somewhat. Park learned how to slide down the side of a mountain on his ass. I told you he was clumsy. We went to the Broadmoor, on the side of a mountain near Colorado Springs, to ski, because it was the only place you could go for a couple hours skiing and not have to make it a weekend trip.

Late in the season, it was basically a huge sheet of ice. As you're looking at the Broadmoor ski slope from the top, it's a long, straight, wide slope, with a few little bumps, but nothing exciting, except for the speed. Remember, it was a sheet of ice. Toward the bottom, it takes about a forty-five-degree dogleg turn to the left. At that turn, if you kept going, which no one sane did, you would hit the moguls. That's a field of large bumps, some of them four feet high, that the advanced skiers use to prove—some damned thing. Anyway, it's just one huge bump after another.

Oh, yeah, remember the thing about *advanced* skiers. So, I was shooting down the slope, doing probably twenty miles an hour, staying on my feet, and Park was behind me, falling back on his ass and yelling, "Yow!" or "Whoa!" every few seconds. I saw the dogleg turn coming up, and I tried to turn. Remember, it was a sheet of ice. The cheap ass skis I'd rented didn't grab. I wasn't turning. Because I was now up on the edges of the skis, accelerating. Oh, and I was not turning. I hit the first mogul. I was up in the air. At twenty miles an hour. I landed the second mogul pretty well, only cracking a bone in my foot. I heard and felt it pop, like a balloon in my foot. I was up in the air again. Still doing twenty miles an hour. I hit the third mogul. Somewhere in mid-air, the sky and ground got transposed, and I was facing backward. I saw Park. He took the first mogul. Also at twenty miles an hour, but he looked like a bundle of cheap nylon ski parkas crossed with an arthritic spider, cause he got skis and poles and legs and arms sticking out every which way, and he was yelling "Yow! Yow! Yow!" And I hit. Sometime a year or so later, I finally slid to a stop, and there was your friendly ski patrol, looking concerned. I heard one say, "I've never seen anyone take moguls that fast." I wanted to tell him he still hadn't, that the moguls took me, but that would have required breathing, and I couldn't do that.

So, I wheezed at him.

Another time, Park, Manny, Freddie, and I were heading back from Vail. It was a "budget" trip. That meant that the four of us slept in my Vega. Four guys in a Vega can keep it pretty warm. On the way home, we got to Castle Rock, and I noticed that we needed gas, so I had everyone dig in their pockets, scrounge under the seats, and come up with all our money for gas.

I don't think I've ever bought thirteen cents worth of gas, before or since.

We ran out of gas when we made the turn into the barracks parking lot.

Skiing wasn't our only off-duty activity. Imagine you have hundreds, no, thousands of young, healthy adults, mostly male, who were in top physical condition and who were used to risky behaviors. There are plenty of dangerous pastimes to keep the horde amused. For my squad, we all decided that we were going to learn how to rock climb. So, we found, I swear to God, an honest to goodness swami. Yup, he lived in the old section of town, and did the whole swami, chanting, robe-wearing, alternative religion thing. But even a swami needs money for the more prosaic needs. His way of making a living in the mundane world was teaching the secrets of rock climbing. He taught us. We were young, in excellent shape, and not afraid of anything, so of course, we did alright. Not well, but acceptable.

When you're climbing, if there's someone down below you and you dislodge a rock, you yell, "Rock!" to let them know there's one coming.

I was climbing a sheer face, about, oh, twenty feet or more above Park, and I had my hand jammed into a crack, and the rock started to crumble. Oh, before I go farther, I need to tell you that I'm a smartass. So, the first rock came loose, and I yelled, "Rock!" The second rock came loose, and I yelled, "Rock!" I came loose, and time slowed down. I fall backward some, but mostly straight down. If I hit Park on the way down, it would be like wiping a booger off your finger onto your, well, someone's, shirt.

So, I yelled. "Rick!"

Told you I was a smartass.

I missed Park.

17

In July 1976, we were on alert duty, and for Fourth of July, the commander threw a party.

When you are on Quick Reaction Force duty, you are confined to the barracks. The requirement (I think, hell, it's been forty-five years!) was to be standing at the parking lot behind the orderly room with our bags, full battle gear, and weapons, within thirty minutes. So, here we were on the bicentennial, and our commander was a pretty good guy. He'd arranged with the mess hall to provide us with burgers and hot dogs and all the fixings for a barbeque. The mess sergeant broke out the big barrel grills, and we had potato salad and coleslaw and "bug juice" drinks. Because this was 1970s, there was a lot of smuggled alcohol around, and the commander allowed wives, children, and girlfriends to attend. Late in the evening, the alarm bell started to ring, and we all cursed a division command that would pull a drill during our down time.

Within forty-five minutes, we were on trucks and leaving the base. Half an hour after that, we were pulling up onto the ramp at Peterson Air Force Base and preparing to load onto an Air Force C-141 transport. Until we started loading, there was a lot of griping and joking about the realism of this drill. I remember that, prior to closing the cargo doors, they loaded at least one pallet of ammunition on it, and someone started saying, "Oh, God, I didn't tell my wife goodbye," which I thought was a pretty silly thing to say. I don't know why, but it made me feel contemptuous of him.

The rest of the next thirteen days is like a photo album in my mind. Try as hard as I might, I can't remember any of the connecting scenes. I'd like to make a story out of those two weeks, but I can't, because the little things that happened that took us from event to event are missing, like so much of my life. I can't make a story out of them, but I'll flip through some of the pages.

I remember when we got to Sharm El Sheikh, Egypt. My God, it was hot. It was just so incredibly hot. We sat on this white concrete aircraft ramp for a day and a half, baking, with sweat just rolling off us, and the commander and the XO were running around trying to get someone to do something for us, and we were just dying. It was so miserable. I told Park that we were in hell. He said, "No, man. Hell is somewhere in Arizona or Texas or some shit. This is just the waiting room."

I remember that now, and it's disturbing how many times he made comments like that in the days to come, like he knew what was going to happen. But he never lost that grin. I see it still, in my dreams. "This is just the waiting room."

He was right.

18

Around midnight, the commander called all the officers and senior NCOs to a meeting. When they got back, we found out where we were going. A country in the Middle East that was always a very Westernized, calm, and friendly place was going through a real meltdown of a civil war. As the anti-government forces began closing in the capital, there were literally thousands of Americans who were suddenly caught with no way out. The city had no real seaport. The civilian airport was out because aircraft were subject to being hijacked, bombed, or blown out of the sky, so airlines were refusing to fly into the city. There were universities with large numbers of American faculty and students. There were businesses and the inevitable tourists, and we needed to get them out.

Back in those days, the buzzword for a period just prior to hostilities was NEO, noncombatant evacuation operations. It was initially setup in the aftermath of the disastrous fall of Saigon and was geared toward getting US citizens and military family members out of Western Europe when the proverbial *Soviet invasion balloon* went up. Also in those days, the US Government was looking for a military "win," so what could be more winning? Here we were, like a whole platoon of Mighty Mice to *save the day*. I mean, after all, no one would fuck with a whole company of heavily armed US infantrymen, so we would just fly in, get the Americans out, and go home. What could possibly go wrong? Well, besides the fact that we were mechanized infantry with no mech, we had no training in urban operations, we had little intel to go on, we were armed to take on a Soviet invasion, and we were totally reliant on the State Department (shudder!) for support.

We landed at the Capital Airport just after dawn, on the eighth of July. It was already hot, and we had no idea where we were. Well, the officers and the first sergeant did, but I remember thinking it was pretty disorienting to not have any idea where we were going and what we were going to do when we got there. At some point during that flight, I vaguely remember wishing that the plane would break down and we would have to return. I didn't know where we were going, but I figured I'd rather be back in Hell's Waiting Room.

Then this Air Force weenie came onto the aircraft and shouted, "Welcome to the Middle East, gentlemen," and Leon Ammando started puking into his helmet.

There were host-nation military trucks parked at the terminal, and within an hour, we were at the embassy. It was a lot of glass and steel and had this big compound surrounded by a wall, but the wall wasn't but two feet high. There was an inner compound that had a huge wall around it, but we soldiers weren't allowed inside there. After all, we might get mud on the floors and not know what salad fork to scratch our asses with.

The outer and inner compound was guarded by Marines, who were not real friendly but were very professional and treated us well. They knew we were getting hosed and were sympathetic, but they had an important job to do, so they literally just didn't have the bandwidth available to help us. We got bunked down, such as it was, and prepared to find out what the hell was going on. No one knew a damned thing. Finally, that night, I guess it was about 2200 hours or so (for you Air

Force types, that would 10 p.m; for the Navy, I believe it would be four bells; for you Marines, Mickey's big hand is on the 12 and his little hand is on the 10), the CO came out and told us what was going on.

It was the first we'd heard of a civil war going on, and it was escalating. Our job was to help get Americans out of the country before they got caught up in it. I remember Park and I looking around while the CO was talking, and Park said, "If this is a war, it's the quietest war there ever was!" Seriously, it was so quiet. We were surrounded by the sounds of a city, and people (women!) walked past us on the street, and everyone was going about their business as normal. I remember us laughing about it. I also remember thinking that the two of us were going to have a good time.

We had to take trucks every day and go out into the city. We went to designated collection points and gathered up Americans, the vast majority of them women and children. We took them to the airport, put them on a US military aircraft, and they left. It was good duty. We'd hear small arms fire sometimes, but in the evening, when the heat broke, we could walk down to the Lido and get falafel and cokes and watch the women. It was pretty cool. That went on for four days. We started to relax some. We'd flirt a little with the women, play with the kids, and sit around in the evenings, feeling the breeze blow in off the sea, laughing and playing cards.

I guess it was on the twelfth or thirteenth that things really started getting out of control. We'd get some wildly inaccurate sniper fire, and a couple of times artillery or rockets would explode nearby, but nothing was close enough to really rattle you. So, we were still pretty relaxed.

We'd gone to the American University and picked up a load of women and children. There were two machine-gunners in the bed of the truck, me and Ronnie. There was a guy with a grenade launcher in the front seat and two automatic riflemen in the bed of the truck, and we had local police gun Jeeps in front of us and behind us. They were some kind of French Jeep, but a Jeep was a Jeep. I don't know why that's suddenly important, but I recall in detail the way the Jeeps looked. I also remember that, typically, the cops in Jeeps were pretty friendly. Normally, we'd sit and talk with them while waiting to get the trucks loaded, trade stuff, bum cigarettes off of each other, and just do that friendly thing that Americans do. This time, though, unlike other times, the cops were really standoffish and wouldn't joke or swap cigarettes or anything. But it was hot, the kids were crying, and we just wanted to get this load done.

There were guys starting to appear in the streets in the last couple of days. We called them Cowboys. They always wore aviator sunglasses, and either jeans or dress slacks and silk shirts. They would have the shirts open down to the third or fourth button and wear a couple of gold chains. They always had a cigarette dangling out of their mouths, the top of a pack of Marlboro's showing from their pocket, and an AK-47 propped up on their hips. They swaggered, and I told Park that, if one of them ever challenged me, I'd show him what the thump gun, my M-60 machine gun, could do.

So much bravado, so little experience.

Anyway, the Cowboys had started to put up roadblocks. They used them for two things: intimidation and crime. They loved the power it gave them when normal people would get out of their way on the streets. They also loved the money, because they would stop people and demand a bribe for the privilege of crossing their turf.

Our commander had gotten into a pissing contest with a bunch of cowboys on the way to the airport the day before, and his police escort had roughed up a couple of them. So, we were told to watch out for the cowboys that day.

We had just picked up about twenty civilians, pretty equal parts women and children, and I think a couple of men. We were on the main ring road that led to the airport, and I was surprised to see the gun Jeep behind us take off and pass us. I wasn't concerned, just surprised. Then I felt the truck slow down as we came to an intersection. I looked ahead of the vehicle and saw there was a cowboy roadblock. Our instructions were to not stop for any roadblocks, so we kept going.

I could see what was happening, and time slowed down.

As we passed the roadblock, I saw these two guys come running out of a store on the corner, both carrying AK-47s. One of them, wearing white pants and a red silk shirt, stopped in the middle of road about 200 or so meters behind us and raised the AK. I was stunned. I mean, who the hell thinks this is a good idea? Then he started firing. And so did I. I was better. I walked the rounds up the street and started hitting him in the torso. His pants turned red from the waistband down in a couple of seconds, and things started flying off him in the back. I hit him with probably four or five or six rounds, because the truck was bouncing, and it was hard to hold the gun on him. I remember thinking that, if I didn't let up on the trigger, the silly son of a bitch wouldn't ever go down. So, I let up, and I saw him hitting the dirt, and I remember seeing his sunglasses bouncing up in the air and his weapon skittering away across the pavement.

I looked down into the bed of the truck and noticed a little girl. Dark hair and huge eyes. And she was screaming because of all the noise. You just don't understand how *LOUD* a machine gun is, and how the muzzle blast just slaps and slaps at you. I remembered that I'd been screaming too. I put my gun down on the tailgate of the truck and sat in the bed and pulled her up into my lap and held on to her and rocked her, telling her it was alright. I don't know who I was trying to convince.

It wasn't alright. She knew that, and I had yet to learn it.

I was telling her that it was alright, but what I was thinking was "I nailed that fucker!" I wanted to go high five people. I felt like a football hero, ignoring the fact that a truckload of civilians watched me cap a dude like it was the most routine thing in the world.

I don't know what happened to that little girl. I hope the memory of gunfire and blood faded over time.

Most days were carbon copies of the day before and it was getting boring. We were sitting around talking with some Marines, and one of my guys popped off with "Man, I wish we'd get some action!"

It was a brilliant Middle Eastern summer morning, the fifteenth of July. We were standing in the chow line in the courtyard of the embassy. We grunts couldn't possibly be allowed into the embassy dining room. After all, we were carrying *guns*! So, some Navy cooks made chow and served it to us in the courtyard. I was standing about three people behind Denny M. when I heard a sound like someone dropped a watermelon on the pavement. I looked around and noticed that one of the cooks was standing there, covered in blood. I thought he'd gotten shot. I moved forward because everyone seemed kind of frozen in place, and I realized that it wasn't the cook. It was Denny. He'd taken a sniper round right where the neck joins the shoulder; it had separated the muscles, now laying on his chest, and he was bleeding. Before my eyes, his white T-shirt turned red, and blood started running over his belt and down his pants. He looked up, and said, "Hey, Hop! I'm going home!" His eyes rolled up in his head, and down he went.

That night, I had my shift on guard and I heard someone come up behind me. It was Park. He asked me what I thought about Denny getting hit, and I told him I didn't know. It was the first lie I ever told Park. I knew. I just didn't want to admit that I was just thinking of that, and that I didn't feel anything. I'd been sitting there, silently crying for my lost conscience, my lost empathy or sympathy for my fellow soldier. I didn't tell Park that everyone else hit the ground when Denny was hit, but Ronnie and I got under the table and ate breakfast. The medics were working on Denny not five feet away. I liked Denny just fine, but it seemed like the thing to do.

After all, I wouldn't want the eggs to get cold.

We'd been taking sniper fire every once in a while, sometimes a couple of times a day, and the commander was about fed up with it. A sniper would get into the apartment building across the street, pop off a couple of rounds at us, and then take off out the back and away into the alleyways.

Except once. This guy took some shots at us, and we all rushed to the wall. I had my gun and Park had the belt fed in, and I was waiting.

Then one of the front doors opened, and out runs this guy. From probably 100 yards away, I don't know who was more surprised, us or him. I think he was more startled, because he came out the front right into us rather than out the back.

He took off running down the street, and man, was he flying. Scared can always run fast. I remember seeing that the soles of his shoes were really light tan. Sergeant H yelled, "Get him, Hop!" So, I stood. I laid the gun sights right on him and, firing thirty pounds of machine gun with a 100-round belt of ammo, from the shoulder, ripped out all 100 rounds. I blew up cars and pavement and windows and didn't hit that fleet little son of a bitch once. Sergeant Huffman shoved me aside, threw his M-16 to his shoulder, and *pop, pop,* and that fleet little son of a bitch went down totally limp.

We went running out to check on him to see if he was wounded, and if he was, to get him to the medics. Except for Huffman. He knew he'd killed the guy.

We got there and rolled him over. One of the rounds had hit him low on the right rear of the skull and exited just above the right eye. It'd blown out the entire side of his head, lifting it up like a bad toupee flying in the wind, but otherwise, his face was just fine. He had the most surprised look on his face, like the last thought that went through his mind was (right after a 5.56 mm bullet) "What the fu—?"

I felt a little woozy, but alright. At least until the Navy medic came running up. He looked at the guy and said, "Hey, look! He sure looks surprised!"

I emptied my breakfast into the street at my feet.

19

The company commander figured that the snipers were infiltrating at night, and to stop them, we needed to put patrols out, also at night. So, at about midnight, a reinforced squad would leave the perimeter, go out onto one of the side streets leading to our area, setup, and wait. Great plan.

My squad went out on the second night. We took trucks out about a mile, then walked for a while. We were in the part of town that had been shelled, a few blocks across the Green Line that divided East and West Beirut, and there was rubble and blocks of concrete everywhere.

We set up in an ambush and hunkered down and waited.

On the walk in, because the ammo for the machine gun is so heavy (700 rounds weighed between fifty-five and sixty pounds), we'd split it up around the squad. No. That's not right. I split it up. My idea. This is important. There will be a test later. Don't worry. It's a pass-fail kind of test.

If you figured out that I failed, you pass.

It was around 2 or 2:30 a.m., when we could hear the sound of shoe soles on dusty concrete. You know, that raspy *ksshhh ksshhh* sound? We still didn't have enough ID on the guys to engage them, but then one of the idiots dropped his weapon. You know what it sounds like when a weapon is dropped. The AK-47 may have a wood stock rather than the plastic one that the M-16 has, but it still sounds like a weapon when it hits the ground.

Something tipped them off, because suddenly, the world just kind of exploded. Suddenly, we were surrounded by bouncing tracers and muzzle flashes, and for a few seconds, there was nothing but the sounds of AKs firing. They weren't hitting anything. Remember, to them, the idea of a war is not to kill the other guy. The idea of a war is to look manly while making a great deal of noise.

The chunk of concrete that I was hiding behind was moving from the impacts. Bullets were hitting the walls behind us, and the sound coming from the weapons was this weird chirping noise that I now know is a characteristic of city combat with modern weapons.

Finally, Sergeant H started shouting, "Open fire, your stupid motherfuckers! Open fucking fire!"

I started servicing targets. See a muzzle flash, lay in three or six rounds, and wait for the next muzzle flash. It was a like two fighters standing toe to toe, swinging away. No one on our side was getting hit. Yet. On their side, though, instead of the *plack plack* of a bullet hitting concrete or brick, every once in a while, you'd hear that hamburger patty sound of it hitting flesh. We were scoring, but not fast enough. We fired, they fired, we fired, and then Park yelled "LOW!"—meaning I had less than twenty rounds left.

Remember, I told you that I'd split up the ammo among the squad? Well, if I was the genius that my mother thinks I am, I would have remembered to retrieve it when we went to ground. I hadn't.

Park offered to go get some more ammo, and I was laughing and said, "Go get 'em!" He jumped up, and I'm unclear on what happened in the next couple of seconds. See, there, I'm doing it again. Notice the change of tone when I hit something I'd rather not talk about. "I'm unclear." Shit. I don't fucking remember much about the next few hours.

I distinctly recall an explosion, like my old friend, the hand grenade. Park stumbled, and suddenly he's out in the street, lying on his stomach.

Oddly, the streetlights were still working, or something must've lit up the streets, because the next few seconds are clear images in my mind.

Park looked up at me with that embarrassed look, and I knew he was thinking that he'd stumbled, again. He started to push himself up in a kind of a half pushup, like he was going to get to his feet, and tracers were flying all around like psychotic lightning bugs. The first round hit him.

It was a tracer, and it hit him in the back, burning through his chest, knocking him to the pavement.

He tried to get up again. The round had gone through his lung, and he coughed this huge spraying fan of blood all over the pavement. I was frozen, and I just sat there and watched. Time slowed way the fuck down, and everything was moving and moving, and he got hit again, this time in the lower back, and I saw his fatigues bunch where he'd been hit. He looked up at me, shouting, but I couldn't hear anything because I was deaf. I sat there as he got hit again, this time a crease across his cheek line, then his head got kinda screwy and warped and he didn't try to get up anymore.

The really painful things are hard to write—like a race to see if I can write it before my mind forces me away from it.

The next thing I remember was Sergeant H throwing me up against a wall and yelling at me to shut the fuck up. Park was dead, and I couldn't bring him back. I guess I was screaming or something.

The sun was coming up. I don't remember the hours in between Park getting killed and the sun coming up. I've tried. Once I went to a hypnotist in California while I was on temporary duty. She told me that some things the mind buries too deeply to retrieve without harm.

I was up against that wall, and there were some of the guys out in the middle of the street. They had a poncho on the ground, and what was left of Park was on it. They had pieces of cardboard and were scooping things up and putting them on the poncho.

They rolled Park up like a cheap cigar, and two of them carried him back to the trucks.

20

The next day was a like a series of snapshots. They put Park on a helo from the Navy carrier offshore. Well, it was Park. It wasn't a body, or even a corpse. It was my best friend. My first confirmed kill. After all, by getting him killed, I might as well have pulled the trigger myself. It oughta be his epitaph. "Killed by his best friend." That'll drive the archeologists nuts!

The company commander took off on a different helo. He just looked at me as the helo lifted, sad, real sad.

I imagined that everyone was talking about me getting Park killed.

I cleaned my gun. I sharpened my knife. I reset all my gear. I taped all the buckles and clips. And I watched the sun cross the sky and go down over the mountains.

Late that evening, Lieutenant D, the executive officer who was in command while the commander was out on the Navy ship, came out and said that the civilian guy from the embassy knew who sent the group out that killed Park. We were going to put together a raid, take them prisoner, and kill any who resisted.

So, there we were. There were only supposed to be ten or so guys in this compound, and we would hit them from two sides at once with an entire platoon and extra machine guns and take them out.

We left after about an hour.

I should have been keyed up or something. Nervous. Antsy. I was still numb. If I knew then what I know now, I would have stayed behind. No, I take that back. I would have known that I shouldn't go, but I was going to kill the pricks who butchered Park.

The compound where these guys lived was supposed to have ten to fifteen guys in it. As we walked on the approach march, I was hyper alert. Now I would know enough to know that I was in blood lust, that I was going to kill somebody, someone was going to have to pay, and it wasn't going to be me, by God. See, if I made someone else pay for killing Park, then obviously it wasn't my fault, was it? WAS IT?

We had no business whatsoever being there, trying what we did.

So, I was outside, covering two sides of the compound, and the other machine gunner, a big blond kid from Minnesota, whose name I can't remember, was covering the other two sides.

The entry teams stacked in near the outside doors, breached the doors, and started entry.

And time slowed down and got that strobe effect. The team would try to make entry, met a hail of fire, back out, then try again and be forced to withdraw. And again. I don't know how many times they tried, and I don't even remember if they ever actually made full entry.

I remember that, but what I don't remember with any continuity is what I was doing. I was searching for targets in windows, but there were people on the streets, and they were all running.

It's only in the last several years that I can really see them. They'd be running, and I was cutting them down. Some here, one there, a couple there. And, when I remember, my soul shrinks, because in my mind, some of them were slender with long hair, and some of them were awful little. I don't know how I know all that detail, because it was darker than the hubs of hell outside that building that night. At some point, there was a tugging on my shirt, and I looked down and behind me and saw a guy on his knees, crying, saying something. "*La.*

La. La" (NO, NO, NO). And I turned the gun and put the muzzle in his face and pulled the trigger and put three rounds in his head, and he got all over me just like a face full of hot mud that smelled like iron and copper and powder residue, and I'm shouting and screaming and shooting and saying shit that I can't remember to this day.

I remember that there were piles of rags in various places in the street as we left. And people were bleeding.

I remember that part. What is funny (if I had a sense of humor) is the fact that I don't remember if we killed or captured anyone in the compound.

But I got my wish. I intended to kill somebody. And I did.

We marched back into the embassy after dawn. There was a Marine Gunnery Sergeant on the gate, and as we came back in, he was standing there, pale as a ghost under his Mideast summer tan, saying, "My God, My God. What did you do? WHAT DID YOU DO?"

You remember that conscience that I told you I was searching for? Well, I hadn't found it yet. I didn't lie to anyone, or to myself. I just refused to think about it. I'm a killer. I killed. What's the problem?

That evening, we went back out again. This time, we were the enemy. There's very little that's faster in a Middle Eastern neighborhood than word of who are the bad guys and who are the good guys. And we were the bad guys.

I wish I could tell you what happened that night, but there's nothing that comes to mind. I don't know that we did anything that I should be ashamed of. I just don't remember.

At some point that night, something hit me in the leg and knocked me down. Then, someone ran a red-hot poker into my calf. I could feel it. I remember after I got shot—laying there and seeing blood in the gutter. My mind wasn't slow then. It was racing. I didn't know where the blood was coming from. I remember vaguely thinking that I was dying. It still amazes me that I was pretty unconcerned, one way or another.

My father went to war and came back a hero.

I went to war and came home in shackles.

The next day, there were these Marines who showed up at the embassy on a helo from one of the ships. They were smiling even less than most Marines, which meant that they wouldn't have even smiled at their mothers.

They called a formation, and we're standing there, and the company commander told us to stack weapons. We were grunts. We did as we were told. Then we marched, by squad, into the embassy, where we were searched, our belts, personal effects, and shoelaces removed. We were shackled, hands to waist, legs to the other guys' legs.

Then, when we were all done, all of Third Platoon, we were marched out to the helo and put on board.

Except for Rick. When they put the shackles on, it hurt like hell because of the bullet hole, so they carried me. Yup. My humiliation wasn't quite complete enough. They carried me.

They took us to the airport where there was an Air Force cargo plane waiting, and we were marched up into it, cuffed to the seats, and off we went.

Air Force to Cyprus. Cyprus to Germany, then to Canada, then back to Peterson Air Force Base, Colorado. The place where 127 boys and men had left mere weeks before. Those people would never come back. Now I know that all of us died in the dusty hell. Park was just the first one.

Then it was the post stockade, where we were quizzed and interrogated and threatened with charges of murder, manslaughter, and other lesser charges. No one would talk. So, there wasn't enough evidence to hold us. After thirty-one days in the stockade, we were released.

The moment when I finally got back, when I went to the apartment that I'd shared with Trudy and saw that it was empty—that moment was clarifying to me. After we were released, I was standing there, and I was just turning, from side to side, trying to make sense of it all. I'd seen all the other guys after we were released, their wives and girlfriends meeting them, and I was standing there with Manny G. I asked Manny what he was going to do, and Manny looked at me for a long moment and said, "I'm gonna find a cab, find a bar, and find out just how much whiskey I can drink," and he walked away without a glance.

So, like an idiot, I caught a taxi and went to the apartment. I don't know what I expected. The door was locked and there was no answer when I knocked, so I went to the apartment office. The lady in the apartment office tried to tell me that Trudy had cleaned the place out a month prior, but I didn't—couldn't—and *wouldn't* believe her, so she showed me. She unlocked the door, and it swung open on an empty apartment. Not a thing in there.

I turned away from that empty place—that apartment that was a house, never a home, and was never to be a home—and I think I realized that it was no emptier than I was. The lady from the apartment office tried to help me as I hobbled from room to room, and she was crying. I don't know why.

I told her I was fine and hobbled my butt out of there.

I don't know where I spent the next few days. It was the first time I'd crawled into a bottle for refuge. I just remember waking up on Mark's living room floor a week or so later. I don't know what happened in that week.

I didn't ask, and they never told me.

The week before Christmas, I was sitting in my room trying to figure out what I was doing. I'd crawled as deeply into a succession of bottles as I could since September, and now I was alone, again, on a Friday night, trying to figure out a way to get some money for another bottle.

Sergeant H walked into my room, and I remember him just standing there, looking at me. I couldn't look up and meet his eyes. I just couldn't. Somewhere, in what little soul I had left, I was awfully ashamed.

He opened my locker and started pawing through the dirty clothes and other shit laying in the bottom. He found my shaving kit and towel and threw them to me and told me to have a shower and shave.

I remember meekly going to shower, and when I looked in the mirror, I was shaving and crying. I don't remember why. There was a lot of that in those months. I was even ashamed of that.

I was pretty much bouncing off the bottom at that point. I don't recall eating very often, and mixing coke in with my rum or vodka had stopped a couple months prior. I stunk, and if it weren't for Mara, a friend's wife (who's a saint), I would have been wearing the same dirty clothes for the last three months.

And watching the slow spin into hell of everyone around me. Vaguely, it was kind of like seeing a bad play, where you don't really pay any attention and just can't wait till intermission.

My new roommate, after Park's death, was Manny.

In November, they found Manny, naked, in front of church in Colorado Springs, praying. When the police were called, he asked them to kill him. Years later, I found out that he'd been committed to a psychiatric hospital in Denver and was catatonic.

Mel had been busted three times for possession of LSD and reds.

Freddy G. was in Canon City Prison for beating his wife and son. His wife spent a month in the hospital from that.

Sergeant Fred just disappeared one night.

Sergeant H2 left to go be the range coordinator and started drinking again. He'd been sober for six years prior to that.

Mark was in an out-patient depression treatment program.

Willie ran off with a thirteen-year-old girl. When they found him, he'd shot himself. Someone said that he still had that stupid grin on his face. I don't know how they'd know, but I like to think that Willie still smiled.

Jimmy went camping one day and didn't come back. I don't know that they ever found him.

The Henrys, that's what we called Henry B and Henry S, got into a fight one night, and Henry S tried to jump out of a window. He made it halfway and disemboweled himself on the broken glass. I don't know if he meant to do that or not. I never told anyone, but someone said he'd become fascinated by the Japanese method of suicide. Henry B refused to talk to the MPs, and Henry S told them that B didn't have anything to do with it. The first sergeant made me and Mango mop up the blood and the shit.

Somewhere along the way, they had a memorial service for Park. It was in the main chapel on base. I refused to go forward to share some "favorite memories of the fallen soldier."

Everyone just turned to look at me, and I walked out. I was unworthy to talk about Park. You don't ask the murderer to share a few kind words at his victim's funeral.

I was sitting outside the chapel when they were done, and they had bagpipes play "Amazing Grace." I squatted there, leaning on the wall, with my heart ripped, shredded, live, and screaming. I thought I was going to pass out.

To this day, the sound of pipes playing "Amazing Grace" makes me cry. I can't help it.

And there I was, crying into the mirror and shaving.

When I got back to the room, Sergeant H told me that I was going to go have dinner with his family and that they were going to have some friends over. He grabbed me on either side of my face and asked me if I could maintain for a couple of hours. He said that there wasn't going to be any booze, not even beer or wine, and that his wife and sons were going to be there. He said that I needed this, but if I couldn't maintain, then he wasn't going to put his family through it. Whatever "it" was.

I started crying again. Not boo-hooing or sobbing or wailing. Just leaking. He grabbed me and held me, then pulled back and said, "Blow your nose, and let's get out of here."

Dinner was incredibly good. I know now that I was on the verge of a complete mental and physical breakdown. If I slept, it was because I was drunk. If I slept, it was for an hour or two at a time. The dreams kept me scared to sleep. The deep, rich, metallic smell of blood, and the weird chirping sound of weapons firing in a city and muzzle flashes strobing the dark. And screaming. Arab voices yelling "*La. La.*" The smell of blood was so powerful, it woke me up; I'd turn on the light and check to see if I was bleeding anywhere.

Sometimes, I'd wake up and sit alone in the dark, listening to the sounds of others reliving hell. Sometimes I'd hear screams, and I couldn't tell if they were in my head or down the hall. That scared me. I wondered if I was going crazy.

I wondered if I was still human.

If I ate, it was usually bar food, or something that someone ordered. To tell you the truth, I don't remember more than one meal between September and December 1976 (the one I remember is Domino's Pizza).

We ate and we talked, and the whole time, Hoskins' dinner guest, this big guy named Paul, was looking at me. I was thinking that Paul might be gay; he was watching me so intently.

When dinner was over, I thanked Mrs. H, and said that I was going to catch a ride back to the barracks, and Sergeant H asked me to stay for coffee and a cigar, so I stayed. It was like I was just a visitor to normal, a tourist, but I was going to experience the whole thing.

We went into Sergeant H's den, and Paul started to talk, and he talked about his own journey. Paul volunteered for the Marines in 1966 and did two and a half tours in Vietnam. I asked him how you do a half tour, and he pulled up his pant leg. His left leg was a prosthetic from above the knee. He knocked on the hollow-sounding plastic and said, "If you forget and leave your leg behind when you pull out, they make you go home."

He started talking about coming home, and I just wanted to get the hell out of there. It was way too close. Kind of the way you feel after you've had your heart broken and you hear a sad country song. All you want to do is turn the radio off. But I was frozen. There were a couple of times when I realized that I was forgetting to breathe. He talked about the day he was wounded, or, as he put it, the day they killed his leg.

He talked about going home and drifting for several years, till he woke in a church shelter in Pueblo, Colorado. He talked about quitting the drugs and the booze and the running and about starting college. Then he told me what his degree was in. He was a licensed counselor and certified to treat what was called "battle stress" at the time.

Then it hit me, and I went off. This wasn't a get-together. This was my first counseling session.

I've found that my extensive vocabulary can be used as a weapon to hurt people. And I tried to hurt him. I even forgot about wanting a drink, and that took some doing in those days. He drove me crazy, sitting there with that half smile on his face, not saying a word. I called him things that would earn me a beating in the barracks. Then I realized that I was crying, and no one could understand a word I was saying as I was talking through the sobs. I wanted to run—oh, God, I wanted to run anywhere to get out of there and not have to think. I wanted a drink or a dozen drinks. I wanted to go where there weren't any people, but I didn't have anywhere to go. I remember thinking that the look on Paul's face must have been like the look on Jesus' face, because there was pain, but it was calm, and there was even a kind of love there, and I didn't want love or sorrow or understanding—I wanted to die, I wanted him to kill me, I wanted anyone to kill me, because I couldn't live with the pain anymore. No more pain. God, please.

I do remember that, in that face, there wasn't any pity. I don't think I could have taken that. I know I couldn't.

I cried myself sick and puked. I cried myself to sleep in that house.

I didn't take another drink for two years.

That wasn't the end of it with Paul. I met with him at least once a week for the next three months. At first, Sergeant H went with me. He said it was moral support, but I think he was on suicide watch. At least I think so now. I wish I'd realized that then. I would have told him that was one thing he didn't have to worry about. I wasn't about to kill myself. I couldn't. There was more pain in my future, and I had to feel it.

Several people have told me that it wasn't my fault that Park died.

Oh, hell, it's time to drop the nice little euphemisms. Park didn't "die." A man who has a heart attack "dies." He topples over and all of him is there, so you can bury him and make some fat mortician in a cheap suit rich.

Park was butchered. He was torn into pieces by the repeated impacts and transits of the pieces of copper-clad lead moving at extremely high velocity through his body. The barbarians who killed them were descended from a rich culture that, for centuries, dominated art and philosophy and science and medicine across most of the known world. They danced and praised God that they won a great victory when they killed this goofy, clumsy, slow-minded, nineteen-year-old boy from Tennessee.

They had to use pieces of cardboard to scoop parts of him into a poncho.

So, I started to say that several people told me it wasn't my fault that Park was torn into shreds.

Several people, my ass.

Everyone who's heard that story—and until now, the list was damned short—has told me it's not my fault. But it was. Because the horrible truth of that night that I've not been able to face is that it was my fault. I loved Park. He was my brother. But he was a little simple. Park was a follower, and that night, I got the crash course in the dark side of leadership when I led Park to his death.

So, yeah, I had to feel the pain.

And I couldn't even do that right.

In March, I had my last session with Paul. I told him that I was alright, that I was on top of it, and that I wouldn't be back; he looked at me with this sadness, told me that I just thought that I was on top of it, but that what I'd actually done is buried it in a shallow grave, that it would get me.

I told him he was wrong.

Oh, God, was he right.

But, you know, my life and career haven't been all about death and blood and tragedy and grand adventures.

There was silly shit, too.

21

I got back to full duty in the late fall of 1976, around November. It just so happens that the first day back on full duty, the unit went to a demolition range.

Those are pretty cool. Basically, the unit splits up into groups, the same number of groups as there are demolition stations. I think the stations were cratering charge, bangalore torpedo, TNT, C4, shaped charge, and improvised incendiary device.

So, off I go with my little group, to the bangalore torpedo station. The bangalore, and God knows where they got that name, is a pipe filled with high explosives. There are little nubs and slots on the ends so you can join them together to make them as long as you want. You put this little rocket nosecone kind of thing on the front, and then you push it under concertina wire and other light obstacles. You initiate the torpedo from the back and run like hell. *BOOM*, and the obstacle disappears, and the Marines take the beach, or something like that.

Then, we go to the cratering charge station. That's an explosive that sits on little legs, with an indentation in the lower middle that causes the explosion to be focused into a jet of force and white-hot gas, used to put craters in runways, ramps, and other pavement-type places to deny the enemy their use. There are other things you can do with them, yes, yes, I know, but that's what they are designed for. There's two, and I think they were twenty pounds and forty pounds. Anyhow, we set it up on hard packed ground, initiated it, and ran like hell. Actually, they tell you to walk. On that range, we walked. In real world, you run. Okay. We initiated it, and then there was the *BOOM*, and a crater, about God knows how many feet deep, and about a foot across, in hard ground and rock. In concrete, it just splinters it. Hell on a runway.

Then, off we go to the incendiary device station. Molotov cocktails. Fire bombs. So, you line up and come up to this pile of bottles and jars. You're supposed to pick up a bottle. They had all kinds there. Beer bottles, wine bottles, ketchup bottles, and one one-gallon mayonnaise jar.

So, guys are looking for their favorite beer bottle, and some of the older guys are going with wine bottles.

But there's this mayonnaise jar. When I get to the pile, I pick it up. There's this engineer sergeant there who says, "Hey, corporal, are you sure you want to use that?" I told him, "Hell, yeah!"

So, I move forward, and there's another engineer sergeant who's got a fifty-gallon drum of gasoline on the back of a Jeep trailer with a hand pump. I take the top off the jar, put it under the spout, and he pumps and pumps and pumps and swears and pumps and swears. And I start getting worried.

Two things were occurring to me.

First, I was gonna have to throw this thing.

Second, a gallon of gas in a glass jar is HEAVY!

But I couldn't back down. I move forward, and a guy there mixes soap flakes into the gas to thicken it. And mixes and mixes and mixes and swears, and finally I say it's good enough.

It wasn't. It was still pretty fluid. Keep note of that.

Well, what we were supposed to do then was take these bombs and go to a tank pulling an old tank hulk around in a circle. The hulk was an old tank with the turret removed. I looked and I was thinking about how I'd throw this thing, and I saw this big old tree next to the circle. It had one big branch that grew out kind of toward the circle. So, there I went.

I climbed up the tree, and holding onto the bomb, I slung my rifle over my back and started to shinny out on the limb. Keep in mind that the limb was about six or eight inches across. I am significantly bigger than six or eight inches across.

I got over to where the hulk was going to be pulled, and I was about ten or twelve feet off the ground. I grabbed the limb with my legs and held the bomb down under the limb, bracing against its underside. I took out my lighter and lit the fuse, and when the tank hulk was under me, I let go.

Instantly, I heard this voice in my head say, "fireball," and I realized what a mistake I'd made. I grabbed the limb with my arms and put my head down against the limb. I was wearing a steel helmet, and they didn't fit worth a damn in those days. When you put your forehead against something, the helmet cocks back on your head, exposing the front half of your skull. I don't remember much about the next few minutes, but I'm told that the bomb hit the tank, and a huge fireball erupted from it, flowing up and engulfing me. They tell me they saw this smoking body come flying out of the flames and impact the ground.

At this point, let's talk a little about clothing and the behavior of fire when it encounters a solid object. First, I was wearing the newest Army fatigues, which were a permanent press, polyester blend. Second, when a flame front hits a solid object—oh, let's say something like a limb—it kinda wraps around it, totally enveloping it.

I lost all the hair on my eyebrows, my mustache, my sideburns, and the hair on my head halfway across my skull. I ended up with flash burns to my face, neck, and hands. The flames half melted my uniform, so it was like having cold plastic armor on and made a shushing sound when I walked.

I learned a lesson that day. I wanted that one-gallon mayonnaise jar. No one else did. The moral of this story is if there's something you want more than anything, and no one else does, there's probably a reason.

My growth—my life as a unique entity called Rick—ended for a long, long time. Once again, I was playing the part. The scriptwriter was me. I looked around, determined what it was that "normal" people did; then I copied them. Monkey see, monkey do. I was like a monkey wearing a tuxedo. You know what you get when you put a tuxedo on a monkey? Just a monkey, but he's better dressed.

I wore that tuxedo for over twenty-five years, till it was frayed and hanging in tatters.

I tried to lose myself in fantasy. I screwed damn near anything in sight, and I know for a fact that, in at least one case, it didn't even have to be sober or conscious.

I met nice girls, and we'd start to hit it off; then I'd do something puzzling to sabotage it.

I met bad girls, and we'd mutually take advantage of each other.

So, along we went. The road taken seemed wrapped in a translucent cloth, and I was just visiting it, rather than living it. The universe didn't care, and I don't think I did either.

I was good at my job. I got rewarded by being a platoon sergeant, in charge of thirty soldiers in an infantry rifle company. It bears repeating here that the Army learned a lot of lessons from Vietnam, and one of them was that there's a place for people who are crappy soldiers when they're not in the field. I had thirty of the biggest liars, thieves, drunks, druggies, and idiots in the world. But damn, they were good when we humped the boonies.

We were part of a light infantry unit. That has a special place in the Army. Light doesn't mean anything. As a unit, you are light because you don't have masses of trucks or tracks to carry you into battle. You had leather personnel carriers—boots. You walked everywhere. You carried everything on your back. We'd march with fifty-pound rucksacks for warm weather operations and eighty to ninety-pound rucksacks for winter operations. Miles. Tens of miles. Once, we marched over 100 kilometers in two days with full winter rucks. There was blood all over the pavement when we walked in the gate. When I took a step, my boots would squish, and blood would come out.

22

I met a woman. Oh, Lord, did I ever. Someone who would put up with my shit and who would let me know when I was full of it. Suddenly, oh so satisfyingly, I had a family, with my wife and her two boys. I was a dad. It was terrifying.

I loved being a father and a husband, but I lived my life in fear of them getting a glimpse of the beast inside of me, and of them learning what I had been and what I'd done. No, I wasn't scared that I would hurt them. I could never do that. The kind of mind that can hurt women or children is completely and utterly alien to me. I don't have a frame of reference for that. As a matter of fact, I can't see how it can ever be justified, and strongly condemn those who commit those kinds of acts. But now I was father to two boys, and I wanted to be a good example for them—show them how to treat everyone, not just women or girls. In the deep recesses of my mind, I just didn't want them to see anything other than the skin that I was wearing, this kind of avatar that I'd adopted.

In between the tough times, there were good times. When we got married, we had combined bills of $150 a month. I made $165 a month. So, we plugged along and made ends meet. Some months, all we had to eat was beans and cornbread. I swallowed the last of my pride and applied for food stamps, which made all the difference in the world. We lived about ten miles, in almost any direction, from some of the best beaches and clearest tropical water in the world. Mokuleia, Haleiwa, Sunset Beach, Pupukea (Shark's Cove), Waimea, on and on. Christmas Day body surfing. Manapua and RC Cola from the Manapua Man on the beach. Stopping at the Dole Pineapple Plantation for a plate of fresh pineapple spears after a day at the beach.

I was a scuba diver, and got my wife certified, and we dove for the next two years. Because I had a lot of experience driving a boat, living by two major rivers, I volunteered to run the dive club's dive boat on weekends—for which they paid me twenty-five dollars a day and gave me free air refills. They paid me to spend all day driving a boat out of Haleiwa or Waianae. *Paid* me.

We dove with dolphins and sea turtles and manta rays the size of motherships. We dove a downed WWII plane off Waianae and dodged flying fish on the way back into harbor. We dropped into eighty-five feet of water off Diamond Head that was so clear I got vertigo, because it looked like there was nothing between me and the bottom. We got investigated by a twenty-five-foot whale shark off Mokuleia and watched a feeding frenzy by white tip reef sharks and dropped into the water during the fall when the gray whales were running to listen to their whale song.

Once we were settled in Hawaii, family life was good. But it was pretty tough duty. You can't imagine how tough. It wasn't uncommon to march the twenty-three miles to the Kahuku Training Area, getting there around 12 p.m. or 2 p.m., set up camp, set the perimeter, then attend a patrol briefing. We'd be out of the perimeter at dusk, moving all night to assault a position or facility, evade pursuit, and come back into the perimeter at dawn. Time for a cup of really, really bad coffee, wolf down a C-ration, then put out recon and security patrols for the day. Along the way, we'd work it so everyone got two hours sleep.

Everyone except the sergeants.

Then we'd do it all over again. Once I went on continual patrol/ briefing/prep/patrol cycle for seventy-five hours straight. Then I screwed up. I sat down. I distinctly remember getting a C-ration, sitting down, and waking up four hours later, after dark, with a poncho over me. I must have gone to sleep as soon as my ass hit the ground. The C-ration and opener (does anyone still remember the P-38?) were still in my hand.

When there was a tough mission in the works, my guys got the nod. When the almost impossible had to happen, we got the mission. Many soldiers in the company came to me wanting to get into my platoon, but my guys, that collection of wayward sons, were unbeatable in the field, and almost unmanageable any other time, but these were my guys, and we didn't need ambitious outsiders screwing up our dynamics. We were good, and we damned well knew it.

I've got a picture around somewhere. It's me and my guys, grouped in front of a helo. Underneath is the name the colonel gave us—Hoppe's Heroes. Yeah, not serious, but definitely tongue-in-cheek, kind of sarcastically.

Sometime in March or April of 1980, I think, we'd been pulling security patrols in Korea just south of the Demilitarized Zone or DMZ. There'd been word of North Korean infiltrators, but hell, we were well south of the DMZ, so there was no problem, right? We came around a ridge, and there were all these Korean soldiers, and they had us dead to rights. They were wearing South Korean uniforms, so we didn't open up on them, but they were way too damned good, and it was starting to worry me a bit, because they never actually pointed weapons at us, but they were always pointed in our general direction.

They escorted us (yes, at gunpoint) back to their command post. They hadn't disarmed us, but they were none too friendly, even as they were working way too hard to convince us that they were just part of the family. I kept exchanging looks with my first and second squad leaders, Dave and Osborne, and we finally got to talk. We figured that we needed to get out of there. If they were actually friendlies, well, they would have to suck up the lack of courtesy. If they weren't friendlies, then we probably were going to die, but maybe some might get clear. The trigger was going to be if they tried to take our weapons; then all bets were off. We would open up, and everyone would scatter and head south, trying to link up with friendlies. We could hear artillery firing to the south, so we figured there was a US firebase somewhere out there, fifteen or twenty kilometers away.

Well, they Koreans sat us down. Out comes their colonel, and he starts asking questions. Just then, a US helo, a Huey, comes over, so I grabbed a red smoke grenade and threw it, and the helo pilot saw it, landed, took us on, and out we went.

Brigade said that there were no friendly units out there. Well, the Koreans didn't kill us, so I guess that they qualified as friendly. After the outbriefing, the colonel looked at us, at me, and said, "Well, do you think you're some kind of heroes? Maybe you are. Hoppe's Heroes!" And so we were. We pulled a lot of patrols during that time and caught a lot of crap from the other squad leaders. But we were heroes. Sort of.

In a change of pace, the company went over to Kaneohe Marine Corps Air Station, on the Windward side of the Oahu. They had the best live fire range, so we spent a day running the lanes back and forth, shooting up a hell of a lot of ammo, and having a hell of a time. We were supposed to spend the night there, and then take trucks back out to Schofield Barracks in the morning.

Me and my A Team Leader, Bill, shared a tent. We were sitting there that night drinking C-ration coffee, and we decided that we should get some booze. Bill and I pooled our money, and we came up with $10. (We were both married. That should explain it.) We sent this one kid, Johnny M, to the Marine Corps Class VI (Liquor) Store, telling him to get as much whiskey as that would buy, thinking, of course, that we were going to get maybe a couple of pints. Everybody would have a touch, and we'd sleep better.

Well, Johnny comes back with a big paper bag. In it are two 1-quart bottles of Club Deluxe Bourbon Whiskey, at four-ninety-five a quart.

I popped one open and took a hit; it was like someone dumped oily napalm down my throat. When I got my voice back, I told Bill that it was hideous, and of course, he had to verify it. He agreed that it was hideous. So hideous that we couldn't allow any of the younger soldiers to have any, because it might rot their brains. So, Bill and me drank the two quarts of Club Deluxe Bourbon Whiskey, chasing it with plastic-tasting canteen water, which somehow went well with it.

I woke the next morning hearing the sun come up over the ocean, like a roaring freight train. I swear I could hear birds breathing. I thought, *Would someone stop those damned ants from tromping around so LOUDLY! MY GOD, I HAD THE WORST HANGOVER!*

We broke camp and packed up. Bill and I were sitting in the morning sun, leaning up against our rucksacks, trying to recover, when we hear a Jeep horn. It's the first sergeant, bringing hot breakfast. Well, lukewarm, after he'd driven it the twenty-five miles from Schofield Barracks.

Bill got up and said that he was going to get something to eat; maybe it'd make him feel better. He asked me if I wanted to go, and I said no, but I gave him my canteen cup and asked him to get me a cup of coffee.

He came back about fifteen minutes later and gave me the cup of coffee. He said he felt better.

A little bit later, I was feeling better. For a few minutes.

We heard the distinctive sound of a flight of Huey helicopters coming in for a landing. I looked at Bill, and Bill sat up straight and said, "They wouldn't!"

You see, the Marines didn't use Hueys. If there was a flight of Hueys there, they were there for one reason and one reason only. To pick us up.

Yup, the commander found a group of Huey pilots who were looking for some extra stick time and convinced them to come get us.

Well, I figured that the helos had to go over the Koolau Mountains, which were about 6,000 or 7,000 feet high. We'd get up that high, and the air would be cool, and we'd feel better.

Oh, no. That just wouldn't do. No. They lifted with us on the birds and started *nap of the earth*. That's a flying technique, where, to avoid radar and anti-aircraft fire, the helo hugs the ground, maybe fifty feet up. The problem with it here, well, was the ground. It was the Koolau's. The ground would rise up at a fifty or sixty-degree angle, 300 or 400 feet high, and the top of the ridgeline wouldn't be but three or four feet across, and the ground would drop at that same angle. Now, imagine doing that at 100 or 120 miles an hour. There isn't a roller coaster in the world that would do that. It's a guaranteed vomit comet.

We dropped down so fast that we were weightless, pulling up so hard that we saw the rotor blades bending, then rising, pulling a couple of gees, and then down again. Time after time.

Now, if you're in a Huey, with a ruck on your back, you're strapped in by the waist, and the ruck makes you lean out of the side of the helo. So, we were there with our knees in the breeze, and I heard something.

I looked to my right, and there was Bill, and his throat was working, and he was gagging. And he hurled.

Bill never did chew his food too well.

So, eggs, coffee, potatoes, bacon, and gravy—oh, yeah, he liked ketchup on his eggs, too. Well, this pink projectile comes flying out of his mouth and goes about thirty feet and almost stops.

Rotor wash.

The projectile went out, stopped, and like it changed its mind, came right back at us.

We called Bill "The Owl," cause when he gets sick, he makes this "*hooooo*" sound. So, it was, "*HOOOO!*" Splatter. "*HOOOO!*" Splatter. "*HOOOO!*" Splatter.

The helo's crew chief is screaming, and puke was getting all over us and inside his helo; the pilots had the windshield wipers smearing the puke across the windshield.

We came into the East Range area, and the helo flared about fifty feet over the landing zone. It started to settle in, and about ten feet off the ground, Bill cut his seat belt loose, hitting the ground in a roll, bouncing back up, running for his life. Right behind him was the crew chief.

The crew chief had on his crew chief helmet, and it had an intercom cable from it to the helo. It was about thirty feet long. It was pretty stout. The crew chief was running for all he was worth when he hit the end of that cable, and it was like a big old Doberman hitting the end of the chain. His head stopped, and his feet came up; then he hit the ground flat.

And Bill was hoofing off into the boonies, rucksack, rifle, and all. And making pretty good time.

We were right behind him. I sure wasn't going to wait around for that pilot to tell me and my guys that they had to clean Bill's puke out of that bird. We got back to the company, and Bill was already gone. They didn't even make us clean our weapons. I walked home, and my wife had me strip out on our covered patio and rinse off with a hose before she let me in the house. I couldn't blame her.

23

I began to relax and for the first time and hope began to creep into my mind. Maybe I could put my past behind me and live a normal life. Maybe pigs will fucking fly, too. I wasn't becoming normal. Hell was just taking an intermission.

But, my mind—my soul—was still kind of locked away. I'd drink too much, but not enough to either remember or forget. I never understood that. I couldn't drink to forget if I was remembering the things that I would rather not. I just drank and counted the cost later. Luckily, I never drank enough to be anything more than a happy drunk, so the kids never saw Dad do anything other than be a little goofy when he drank.

On and on it went. Training deployments to New Zealand (think sleeping in a pile of sheep shit in a freezer—that's New Zealand's Waiourou Training Center). Australia, marching up and down Lever Plateau with the 1st Royal Australian Regiment diggers and drinking XXXX beer. Korea again, damn soju and Coke—shudder. Pohakaloa Training Area on the Big Island where I had a good pair of combat boots torn off my feet by old lava flows.

Then, during the middle of the night on a patrol base in the Kahuku

Training Area, I realized that I had to make a change. As a sergeant, I realized that all I had to look forward to was making an ever-increasing number of people do things that they didn't want to do, all while my body was breaking down. After a field exercise, my knees would be swollen to the size of grapefruits. I'd picked up a systemic fungal infection in Panama that would just pop up from time to time. Too many years around machine guns and other things that go *boom* left me with mid and high-range hearing loss. Too many years humping long distances carrying heavy loads was compressing my spine, and I was getting nerve issues. And I was only twenty-six years old.

A couple days later, I was out in front of the company catching a smoke and thinking about my predicament. I'd been to see the reenlistment NCO and was told that about the only thing open for reclassifying from infantry was computer programming. I was thinking about being a computer programmer, and I remember that it sounded incredibly boring, and that was even if I managed to make it through training, and that was far from guaranteed. "But, but, Rick, you're an intelligent guy!" Well, that may be. I'm not saying it, but I will tell you that it took three tries to get through freshman algebra in college, and even I knew that you had to have a good grasp of math to be a programmer.

I guess you could say I was *pensive*. I was brooding and feeling a bit sorry for myself. I realized someone was talking to me and looked over to see the company commander standing there. He asked what was on my mind, and I opened up to him. He and I had always gotten along really well—well, except for the time that I accidentally detonated a booby trap in Korea and put the whole company on alert until I fessed up. Anyway, our company commander was a former intelligence officer and had been part of the Phoenix Program in Vietnam, so he had some background other than infantry.

I was about a year out from the end of my hitch, and we'd just welcomed our third child into the family. I'd deployed to Korea for an exercise and returned on April 13. On April 15, my wife went into labor at 3:29 p.m. It took us about ten minutes to get to the on-base clinic, and they realized that she was very, very close to delivering, so they put her in an ambulance to take her to the helo pad for a Medevac flight to Tripler Army Hospital in Honolulu. We had to wait for the physician's assistant and were sitting in the ambulance outside the clinic when my wife had her second labor pain and gave a wail. Beast didn't like that, and I turned to the ambulance driver and said, "Get this fucking thing moving or I'm gonna start tearing things apart." The sure way to get me from reasonable to Beast mode was to screw with my family. The driver called into the clinic and told them we were moving, and at that minute, the physician's assistant came flying out of the door with his bag. We got to the helo pad and the bird was already spinning up. I fell back on my training and helped get my wife into the helo, and off we went. Just about fifty feet off the pad at the hospital, as we were flaring out to land, in the middle of a tropical rainstorm, my wife had her third and final labor pain, and suddenly there was this little human in our midst. I was told later that the pilot called into the hospital and told them to change our passenger count from three to four, saying, "And it's a girl!" As they loaded my wife into the ambulance, I shook the crew chief's hand, the pilot's and co-pilot's hands, the ground crew's hand—hell, I would have shaken the helo's hand if it had one.

And then we were five.

24

I realized that I was a good grunt, whatever the hell that meant, but I had no skills other than to take orders and do impossibly physical things to the detriment of my health, with a wife and three children to provide for. Don't get me wrong. I loved being a grunt, especially being a leader of soldiers. But I was falling apart. I had to do something else. I told the commander what was going on and he just said, "Come with me." He took me to Battalion reenlistment and told them to get me into a reenlistment and reclassification program called "BEAR" (bonus enlistment and reclassification), so I could become a counterintelligence agent. I had no idea what a counterintelligence agent did, but such was my trust in this particular commander that I just went along with his recommendation. To this day, I thank God that Captain G was on my side.

The process to become a counterintelligence (CI) agent is long and involved. There are interviews and essays and a background investigation that was the administrative equivalent of a colonoscopy. In the back of my mind, though, I remembered a month in the stockade, and charges dropped but not forgotten. I was figuratively hunched over, waiting for the call that would say, "Unfortunately, we are unable to complete your application process at this time. We wish you well in your future . . . blah blah blah."

It never came. Instead, I got a call that I was to go get a photo taken of me in civilian clothes, which of course meant a suit and tie. I didn't own a suit and tie. Hell, I'd never even worn a suit in my life. Infantrymen are not known as fashionistas, but I found a friend who was my size, and I showed up for my photo in the most God-awful suit. I didn't even realize it was so bad—some kind of polyester nightmare with a weird brown and black pattern to it—but I was wearing a suit and a tie, so that was good enough for me. Evidently, whatever deliberating body was responsible for reviewing the applications was used to infantrymen and their *interesting* clothing choices. The day came when I was notified that I was selected for CI agent training, and we began preparing to leave Hawaii.

A few months before our departure date, I spoke with my wife about wanting to adopt her two boys. They weren't my stepsons. They were my sons, but with different last names; they would always be looked at as different, somehow. These were my boys, and the Beast didn't like it when someone slighted my boys.

Three days before we left the islands, we were in Honolulu District Court and walked out with the adoption decree for my oldest son. Two days later, about twelve hours before we left the islands, we did the same with my youngest son. I can't tell you how proud I was. And it was the first time ever that I found a place where I could be alone and allowed myself to cry tears of happiness.

I felt myself healing and becoming more . . . me. I still had nightmares, and still only slept four or five hours a night. But I was, somehow, better. Or I thought I was. The tuxedo fit that monkey like a glove, but the terrors and the fear and the pervasive, continual anger just wouldn't go away! I'd tamp it back down, and it would pop back up a day or a week or a month later.

What kept me going was that I had something to live for. I had people who loved me and counted on me, and who I loved and would do anything for. I wasn't happy that this meant I was to live with the fear and even a bit of loathing, but that was the price to pay for a meaningful life.

I was to live my life on the edges of society. I'm not griping. It's just true. I'm on the periphery. I'm inconvenient. I have big feelings. Passions, even. And those are inconvenient. I've already said it; most people can't do different. I'm *different*. I'm not saying that I'm better. I'm just way different.

People want settled. People want predictable. People want routine. People want lives of quiet contemplation, and lives without disquieting confrontation.

I want neither, nor have I achieved such a state. To love me is to be inconvenienced.

When your highs are this high, you can't help but have some lows. But most people can't handle that. They want to cherry-pick. They want to take the good and flee when the bad happens. Well, except for one person. Thank God for her. Thank God she stuck around. You know what it's like to hit bottom? Not just hit bottom, but to hit so hard you get imbedded in the bottom? You get stuck there, like in a glue trap, and you can't even raise a hand, or lift your head? Where everyone is better than you, because they're not stuck on the bottom? I found out.

You're in so deep that you can't even feel pain. Everything is painful, but it feels like it is pain that's happening to someone else, and you are being forced to watch it. Everyone talks around you, and you catch them looking at you out of the corner of your eye. Their concern is infuriating, but your fury is as maddening as the pain because you can't even embrace it.

Well, that's another story, and it may yet take me another thirty years to face that.

I heard a song by Chris LeDoux once. The refrain was something like, "Live like you ain't afraid to die. And don't be scared, just enjoy your ride. Keep your eyes fixed where the trail meets the sky." Yeah.

That's me. I'm still looking out at the horizon. I realized, though, that it's not the destination. It's the journey.

And here I am. I've looked at my soul, and it's looking back at me. At this point, I'm supposed to say that I've overcome my hatred of myself, that I'm a good man, and I'm all better now. Can I have some fucking ice cream? But I've not lied throughout this story, and I won't now.

I'm still the guy who got his best friend killed. I'm still the guy who can kill, easily and without remorse. I'm still the guy who can kill and be pissed at the victim. I can't change that.

But I can say without reservation that I know who and what I am. I've been forced into it. God, through the agency of other people, grabbed my face and held me up to the mirror. It was a matter of introducing myself or running forever into the darkness and waiting for the end.

I don't know what part God has played in this, or perhaps his adversary played a bigger role. I don't know for sure which side I've been playing on. I like to think I'm on the side of the angels.

So, I started this tale off talking not about self-hatred but about fear. I'm no longer afraid to peek at myself. At times, I almost catch myself swaggering, that how cocky I'm feeling. I've lived in this bubble, a hell of my own making, and the last bits of its rotting remnants are dropping away, and I find a guy who's more like, well, other guys, and is still unique.

I find myself spending time around co-workers, and they will seek me out to spend time with me, this broad diversity of people, and we laugh and joke and have a good time and call each other "brother" and "sister." And mean it. I spend some time with myself, reading or thinking or riding my bike, and I don't feel alone.

So, if all that's so rosy, what about fear? There is still that one thing that I fear, a deep abiding fear. But both the Beast and I are getting older. Time will tell if I get over it. Maybe I won't. Who knows?

What I can say is this.

There's a lot more stops on this journey. Trust me, no one else wants on this wagon, but by God, I'm going to drive it till the wheels fall off, and then I'm gonna walk, and when I can't walk, I'm gonna crawl, and when I can't crawl, well, like the man says, I'm gonna find someone who can carry me. At the end, standing there at the edge of eternity, I hope I get to make my case. I've got friends to meet. I'm afraid most of them won't be where I'm going.

But maybe, just maybe, I've been on the side of the angels all along.

ACKNOWLEDGMENTS

Writing a book is harder than I thought and more rewarding than I could have ever imagined. Due to security concerns, and to protect those who have been hurt enough, so much has had to be changed. The events and people are real; the locations of some and the names of most are not. It was cathartic, and so very hard to write, but I'm glad I did.

None of this would have been possible without the tolerance (usually) of my friends and family.

Through my recovery from PTSD, my late wife, Carolyn, stood by me (not an easy thing to do) and, with a touch, could bring me gently and peacefully out of the worst nightmares. She didn't live to see the publication of this book, but I feel her around me, and I know that she is thinking, *It's about time! I knew you could do it!* Her support was unwavering, her love was unconditional, and she was the glue that held this family together.

I'm eternally grateful for the love and support of my children. Robert, who has no idea how truly brilliant he is and doesn't give himself enough credit for being an amazing father and husband, and still tolerates my periodic calls for technical support. Andrew, who epitomizes the saying, "There's just no stopping a man who is in the right and just won't quit!" Life keeps knocking him back, but never knocks him down. Jenna, who is a true intellectual and lifelong learner, with that rare ability to put academic learning into daily reality. She is the prime example of warrior, woman, steadfast wife, and nurturing mother.

To my grandchildren, Natasha, Tia, Ian, Drew, and Matthew, you make me laugh with your humor and make me cry happy tears with your love. Thank you.

To my daughter-in-law, Stephanie, and son-in-law, Joshua, thanks for being the incredible, talented, compassionate, and loving people you are, for loving me despite the obvious drawbacks.

I've been extraordinarily fortunate to have the friends that I do, who put up with my moods, tolerate my sense of humor, and who stand with me for every step of the way. Bruce, thanks for not firing me so we could have drinks on the roof of that hotel in Kiev! Jeff, thank you for not getting in a firefight in Kabul when we were on our way to the restaurant, especially because the other guys were two Kabul Police technicals with RPDs mounted on them. Also, I must recognize you for being the only guy who can call me "Old Man" and mean it as a gesture of respect. Charlie, my "much" younger brother in arms, we eventually will go for that motorcycle vacation in Gatlinburg! Daniel, we've been through some stuff, haven't we? And don't think I've forgotten that you owe me a bottle of Basil Hayden's! And others who I am forgetting to mention, but who will be sure to let me know!

To my mother and father, Jane and Melvin, who never got to see this book, but wouldn't be surprised. To my sisters, Kathy, Elizabeth, and Vicki, I'm reminded of a quote from somewhere. *I smile, because we're family. I laugh, because there's not a darned thing you can do about it.* Kathy never got to see this book, either, but she set the standard for how a Hoppe fights for the ones they love.

To my cousin, Dennis, we couldn't be closer than we are, even had we been born of the same mother and father. And, can you believe, after all the crap we pulled, we're still alive and not in jail! I mean, thank you.

To Coach (later Principal) Richard Sandoval, who taught me that "cool" wasn't something you cultivated. "Cool" was what you are when you are completely honest with yourself and the world.

I want to express my profound gratitude to John Koehler and the entire crew at Koehler Books. Miranda Dillon, Joe Coccaro, Kellie Emery, and more, who I will undoubtedly forget to mention, but to whom I will owe an adult beverage and a sincere apology in my next book. Thank you for shepherding me through this process and showing patience in tandem with your obvious talent and expertise.

Writing a book about your life is a daunting process, especially when security concerns make you obscure many details. For those who want to know more about locations and events, I apologize, but what you see is what you get. I'm not writing the history of those locations, but my life travels through those events and places. If I had included all the details, there is no possibility that the Department of Defense would pass the book through security review.

And, finally, to my partner, Alice, who gives me her friendship, support, and bubble-bursting, as needed, and never fails to encourage me.

CPSIA information can be obtained
at www.ICGtesting.com
Printed in the USA
LVHW042201120722
723217LV00006B/267